Introduction to Programming in C++

A Laboratory Course

INTRODUCTION TO PROGRAMMING IN C++

A LABORATORY COURSE

JAMES ROBERGÉ

GEORGE SMITH

Illinois Institute of Technology

Jones and Bartlett Publishers

Sudbury, Massachusetts

Boston London Singapore

Editorial, Sales, and Customer Service Offices
Jones and Bartlett Publishers
40 Tall Pine Drive
Sudbury, MA 01776
(978) 443-5000
(800) 832-0034
info@jbpub.com
http://www.jbpub.com

Jones and Bartlett Publishers International
Barb House, Barb Mews
London W6 7PA
UK

ISBN 0-7637-0312-5

Printed in the United States of America

00 99 98 97 10 9 8 7 6

To my grandparents,
for showing me what strength is

- J.R.

To my family and friends,
for their unconditional love and support

- G.K.S.

Introduction to Programming in C++ A Laboratory Course Program Disk

Jones and Bartlett Publishers offers free to students and instructors a program disk with all the complete programs found in *Introduction to Programming in C++ A Laboratory Course*. The program disk is available through the Jones and Bartlett World Wide Web site on the Internet.*

Download Instructions

1. Connect to the Jones and Bartlett student diskette home page **(http://www.jbpub.com/disks/)**.

2. Choose *Introduction to Programming in C++ A Laboratory Course.*

3. Follow the instructions for downloading and saving the *Introduction to Programming in C++ A Laboratory Course.*

4. If you need assistance downloading a Jones and Bartlett student diskette, please send e-mail to help@jbpub.com.

*Downloading the *Introduction to Programming in C++ A Laboratory Course* program disk via the Jones and Bartlett home page requires access to the Internet and a World Wide Web browser such as Netscape Navigator or Microsoft Internet Explorer. Instructors at schools without Internet access may call 1-800-832-0034 and request a copy of the program disk. Jones and Bartlett grants adopters of *Introduction to Programming in C++ A Laboratory Course* the right to duplicate copies of the program disk or to store the files on any stand-alone computer or network.

To the Student

Objectives

We feel strongly that in order to learn a subject, you need to immerse yourself in it—learning by doing rather than by simply observing. We also believe that computer science is more than programming—it is using programming as a tool to create solutions to challenging problems. This emphasis on hands-on learning is used throughout *Introduction to Programming in C++: A Laboratory Course.* In each laboratory, you create programs that apply a particular language feature. As you create these programs, you learn how C++ works and how it can be applied. The resulting programs are working pieces of software that you can use in later laboratories and programming projects.

Organization of the Laboratories

Each laboratory consists of four parts: Prelab, Bridge, In-lab, and Postlab. The **Prelab** Exercises are a homework assignment. Each Prelab Exercise includes a background section that introduces a programming technique and the associated C++ language constructs, a Warm-up Exercise in which you complete a "fill-in-the-blank" problem to practice the syntactic details of the language constructs, and an Application Exercise in which you apply the programming technique to solve an interesting real-world problem.

In the **Bridge** Exercise, you test and debug the software that you created in the Prelab Application Exercise. In the **In-lab** Exercise, you extend or apply the concepts introduced in the Prelab. The last phase of each laboratory, the **Postlab** Exercise, is a homework assignment in which you analyze a program, programming technique, or language construct.

Your instructor will specify the exercises you need to complete for each laboratory. Be sure to check whether your instructor wants you to complete the Bridge Exercise prior to your lab session or during lab. Use the cover sheet provided with each laboratory to keep track of the exercises you have been assigned.

Student Disk

The Program Disk accompanying this manual contains a set of tools that make it easier for you to create programs. These tools include programs discussed in the background sections,

program shells for the Warm-up Exercises, test programs, and data files. The file *read.me* lists the files used in each laboratory. As you read a laboratory exercise, look for the floppy disk icon in the left margin. This icon indicates that the text is referring to a file on the Student Disk. You will need to use this file in order to complete the exercise. The floppy disk icon next to this paragraph, for example, is signaling you to look at the *read.me* file.

To the Instructor

Objectives

Two years ago, we began the process of switching our CS1 and CS2 courses from Pascal to C++. As C and C++ have a reputation for being difficult to learn as a "first language," many of our colleagues were somewhat skeptical about this change. Their concerns were lessened, however, when they realized that we were adopting the same lab-based approach we had used successfully in the Pascal versions of these courses. If our efforts in converting our courses to C++ are any indication, a laboratory experience is essential if students are to get the hands-on experience and feedback they need to succeed as C++ programmers.

The exercises in this book use the laboratory to involve students as active, creative partners in the learning process. By making the laboratories the focal point of the course, we sought to immerse students in the course material. We wanted to challenge them and yet provide the structure, feedback, and support that they needed to meet the challenge. We sought to create programming exercises that are practical and pedagogically sound, and that focus on novel applications rather than simply reconstituting exercises that have survived since the "Dawn of the Computer Age." The resulting exercises are well-defined, yet open-ended enough to allow the better students to do some exploring.

Organization of the Laboratories

When we first began using laboratories, we attempted to shoehorn the creative process into a series of two-hour closed laboratories. The result was a pressure cooker that challenged everyone but helped no one. In experimenting with solutions to this problem, we developed a laboratory framework that retains the creative element but shifts the time-intensive aspects outside of the laboratory period. Within this structure, each laboratory consists of four parts: Prelab, Bridge, In-lab, and Postlab.

PRELAB

The Prelab Exercises are a homework assignment that bridges the gap between the lecture and the laboratory session. In the Prelab Exercises, students explore and create on their own, and at their own pace. Their goal is to synthesize the information they learn in lecture with material from their textbook to produce a set of programs. Each Prelab Exercise includes a background section that introduces a programming technique and the associated C++ language constructs, a Warm-up Exercise in which the students complete a "fill-in-the-blank" problem to practice the syntactic details of the language constructs, and an Application Exercise in which the students apply the programming technique to solve an interesting real-world problem. The entire Prelab assignment—including a review of the relevant lecture and textbook materials—typically takes five to six hours to complete.

BRIDGE

The Bridge Exercise asks students to test and debug the software that they developed in the Prelab Application Exercises. The students use a test plan they developed in the Prelab to evaluate their code. This exercise provides an opportunity for students to evaluate their Prelab work and to resolve any difficulties they might have encountered. The students especially appreciate the feedback they get from the lab instructors regarding the design, structure, and efficiency of their programs.

IN-LAB

The In-lab assignment takes place during the laboratory session proper (assuming that you are using a closed laboratory setting). Each In-lab consists of two exercises that extend or apply the concepts covered in the Prelab. Most students will not be able to complete both In-lab Exercises within a typical closed laboratory period. We have provided a range of exercises so that you can select those that best suit your laboratory environment and your students' needs. An individual In-lab Exercise typically takes about one hour to complete.

POSTLAB

The last phase of each laboratory is a homework assignment that is done following the laboratory session. In the Postlab Exercise, students are asked to prepare a written analysis of a program, programming technique, or language construct. Each Postlab Exercise should take roughly thirty minutes to complete.

Using the Four-Part Organization in Your Laboratory Environment

The term *laboratory* is used by computer science instructors to denote a broad range of environments. In our courses, for example, one group of students attends a closed two-hour laboratory. At the same time, another group of students takes the class via a television network and "attends" an open laboratory. In developing this manual, we tried to create a laboratory format suitable for a variety of open and closed laboratory settings. How you use the four-part organization depends on your laboratory environment.

Two-Hour Closed Laboratory Session

Prelab
We expect the students attending a two-hour closed laboratory to make a good-faith effort to complete the Prelab Application Exercises before coming to lab. Their work need not be perfect, but the effort must be real (roughly 80 percent correct).

Bridge
We ask students to complete test plans for their Prelab work and to begin the testing and debugging process specified in the Bridge Exercise before they come to lab (as part of the 80 percent correct guideline).

In-Lab
We use the first hour of the laboratory session to resolve any problems the students might have experienced in completing the Prelab and Bridge Exercises. Our intention is to give constructive feedback so that students leave the lab with working Prelab software—a significant accomplishment on their part.

During the second hour, we have students complete one of the In-lab Exercises to reinforce the concepts learned in the Prelab. You can choose the exercise by section or by student, or you can let the students decide which one to complete. Students leave the lab having received feedback on their Prelab and In-lab work. You need not rigidly enforce the hourly divisions; a mix of activities keeps everyone interested and motivated.

Postlab
After the lab, the students complete the Postlab Exercise and turn it in at the beginning of the next laboratory session.

One-Hour Closed Laboratory Session

Prelab
When we have only one hour for the closed laboratory, we ask the students to complete both the Prelab and Bridge Exercises before coming to lab. This work is turned in at the start of the laboratory period.

In-Lab
During the laboratory period, the students complete one of the In-lab Exercises.

Postlab
Again, the students complete the Postlab Exercise and submit it at the beginning of the next laboratory period.

OPEN LABORATORY

In an open laboratory setting, we have the students complete the Prelab Exercise, the Bridge Exercise, one of the In-lab Exercises, and the Postlab Exercise. You can stagger submission of these exercises throughout the week or have the students submit the entire laboratory as a unit.

ORDER OF TOPICS

Laboratories 1 through 9 cover the essence of programming in C++. These labs build on each other in terms of content. In selected, well-identified cases, a laboratory may reuse code from a previous lab. Laboratories 10 through 13 cover a variety of advanced topics. You may assign these labs in whole or ask the students to do individual exercises depending on your course emphasis and time constraints.

LABORATORY 14: TEAM SOFTWARE DEVELOPMENT PROJECT

In the Prelab Application Exercises, each student works as the sole developer of a well-specified program. However, it is also important to introduce students to problems that are broader in scope. Laboratory 14 is multiweek programming project in which students work in teams to solve a more open-ended problem. During the first week, the teams analyze a problem in terms of objects and develop a design for the problem. During the second week, they create and test an implementation based on their design.

Laboratory 14 begins by walking the students through the design and implementation of a simple children's calculator program. The software development framework used in this example stresses object-oriented design/programming, iterative code development, and systematic testing. The students then apply this framework to the solution of a more challenging—and more interesting—problem. The laboratory exercises structure the dynamics of the team software development process.

Note that you can use the problem provided, or you can substitute a problem of your own simply by replacing one page in the laboratory. Note also that you can assign this laboratory as an individual project simply by giving the students more time to complete the project.

GRADING

We do not view quantifying student performance to be the primary goal of the laboratory assignments. Students who work hard and master the material covered in the labs are better prepared for exams and, as a result, tend to perform better on exams. Once students realize that the labs are the most important part of the course—yes, even more important than our lectures—and that they learn a great deal from the laboratory assignments, we have little trouble getting our students to complete their lab assignments. Grades do seem to provide needed motivation for some students, however, and for this reason we grade the laboratory exercises. Our grading standards for the labs are designed to reflect effort as much as results.

We view the Prelab Warm-up Exercises as preparatory work and do not formally grade them. During the lab, the lab instructor executes each Prelab Application Exercise using selected test cases. If problems are discovered, the instructor reviews them with the student and the student is given an opportunity to make corrections based on this feedback. The same is true for the assigned In-lab Exercise. Postlab Exercises are graded outside of lab.

Instructor Disk

An Instructor Disk containing solutions to all the Prelab and In-lab Exercises is available on request from Jones and Bartlett Publishers.

Comments and Suggestions

We are very interested in receiving feedback on this manual. Send your comments and suggestions to either of the following e-mail addresses:

csroberge@iit.edu
cssmith@iit.edu

Acknowledgments

We would like to thank our editors at D. C. Heath—Randall Adams, Karen Jolie, and Celena Sun—for their support and encouragement. They saw the potential in this project, and their vision and advice helped guide it to completion. We also would like to thank Keith B. Olsen at Montana Tech, University of Montana for reviewing the manuscript.

We are also grateful to Steve Jackson, Rich McKnight, Chris Merrill, Jami Montgomery, Floyd Saner, Wen Leu, Ana Sanchez, Mauricio Silva, Sudnya Sukthankar, Kuang Wu, Aruna Yeduguri, Cheryl Hyman, Agastya Kohli, Natalie Linden, Fahed Riaz, and the many CS 200 students for their comments on earlier drafts of these laboratories.

Many thanks to Bob Carlson and Charlie Bauer for establishing the curriculum initiative and laboratory infrastructure that made this project possible.

J.R.
G.K.S.

Contents

Getting Your Feet Wet

OVERVIEW

Before starting any project, you need to become familiar with the tools and resources that you have at your disposal. In the context of writing computer programs, these tools and resources are referred to as the **program development environment**. In this laboratory you explore compiling and debugging tools and resources available in your program development environment.

In the Prelab Exercise you create a Quick Reference Survival Guide—a list of frequently performed activities and functions in your environment. You complete the Survival Guide by writing the steps—commands, keystrokes, and mouse actions—needed to perform each function.

You begin a hands-on tour of your program development environment in the Bridge Exercise by compiling, linking, and running (executing) a sample C++ program. This program explains the origin of the name C++ and makes you part of the story. You explore several features of the editor by modifying the program to include a story about "smiley." :–)

The tour continues as you use some of the more common tools for source-level debugging. You examine how a computer program can guess your age by using breakpoints and variable watches to track changes in the value of a variable as the program executes. Your tour concludes with an introduction to the types of errors you encounter as a programmer. You use the debugging tools you have studied to help you fix a program that contains a syntax error and a logic error.

LABORATORY 1: Cover Sheet

Date .... Section ....

Name ....

Place a checkmark in the *Assigned* column next to the exercises that your instructor has assigned to you. Have this sheet ready when your lab instructor checks your work. If your exercises are being checked outside the laboratory session, attach this sheet to the front of the packet of materials that you submit.

Exercise		*Assigned*	*Completed*
Prelab	Touring Your C++ Environment		
Bridge	Editing and Executing C++ Programs		
In-lab 1	Debugging Your Programs		
In-lab 2	Syntactic and Logic Errors		
Postlab	Error Analysis		
		Total	

Laboratory 1: Prelab Exercise

TOURING YOUR C++ ENVIRONMENT

Date .... Section ....

Name ....

BACKGROUND

Many software packages include a keyboard template or reference card that lists frequently used commands and functions along with the steps required to execute each command or function. You can use this card for quick reference instead of looking up a command in a manual or accessing on-line help. In this exercise you create your own Quick Reference Survival Guide—a list of commonly used commands and functions in your C++ program development environment.

QUICK REFERENCE SURVIVAL GUIDE

The following two pages outline various functions that you need to perform when creating a program. For each function, list the commands, keystrokes, or mouse actions needed to perform the function. Space is provided after each section for additional functions that you find useful. Use any available resources that describe your environment's operating system, editor, compiler, and debugger (if available)—possible resources include user's manuals, on-line help, or a system tutorial.

Quick Reference Survival Guide

SYSTEM LEVEL FILE USE

Open a file for editing

Display the contents of a file

Copy a file to a different disk or directory

Rename a file

List the names of the files stored on a disk or in a directory

Print the contents of a file

EDITING A FILE

Go left one character

Go right one character

Go up one line

Go down one line

Go to the beginning of the file

Go to the end of the file

Go to the beginning of the current line

Go to the end of the current line

Insert a character

Delete a character

Insert a line

Delete a line

Delete multiple lines

Move multiple lines to a new location in the file

Save the file

Save the file with a new name

PROGRAM EXECUTION

Compile a program *

Link object files *

Run a program

View program output

* On some systems, compiling, linking, and/or running are performed as a single step.

DEBUGGING DURING PROGRAM EXECUTION (IF AVAILABLE)

Trace program execution line by line (stepping through a program)

Set a breakpoint at a specific line

Remove a breakpoint

Set a watch on a variable

Remove a watch

mark block begin Ctrl-K B
" " end " K

move block

Laboratory 1: In-lab Exercise 1

DEBUGGING YOUR PROGRAMS

Date .... Section ....

Name ....

In order to find the mistakes (or "bugs") in your programs, you often need to execute a program line by line. Many program development environments include **debugging** features that allow you to step through a program and watch the values of variables change as the program executes. Tracing through a long program in this way can become very tedious. Often you are interested only in what is occurring beginning at a certain point in the program. You can signal the debugger to stop execution at a particular line by setting a **breakpoint** at that line. When you run the program, execution stops at the breakpoint. You then can set **watches** on selected variables and step through the rest of the program examining changes in the contents of the variables as the program executes. If your program development environment does not have a debugger, you can check how a program is functioning by outputting intermediate results throughout the program.

STEP-BY-STEP, INCH-BY-INCH

In this exercise you examine the execution of the following program from the file *guessage.cpp*.

```
// Determines a person's age based on a "magic" number.

#include <iostream.h>

void main ()
{
    int num;

    // Explain how to compute a "magic" number.
    cout << endl;
    cout << "I can guess your age from a magic number that "
         << "you compute as follows:" << endl;
    cout << "  1. Add 21 to your age." << endl;
    cout << "  2. Double the result of step 1." << endl;
    cout << "  3. Add your age to the result of step 2." << endl;
    cout << "  4. Subtract 18 from the result of step 3." << endl;

    // Prompt the user for the magic number and read the number from
    // the keyboard.
    cout << "Enter your magic number: ";
    cin >> num;
```

```
    // Compute the user's age.
    num = num / 3;
    num = num - 8;

    // Output the user's age.
    cout << "You are " << num << "."<< endl;
}
```

VERSION A: USE IF A DEBUGGER IS AVAILABLE.

Step 1: Set a breakpoint at the following line.

```
cin >> num;
```

Step 2: Run *guessage.cpp*. Note that execution stops at the point where the breakpoint was set.

Step 3: Set a watch on the variable num.

Step 4: Step to the next line and enter your magic number.

Step 5: What value is now stored in num?

num: ________

Step 6: Step to the next line. What value is now stored in num?

num: ________

Step 7: Step to the next line. What value is now stored in num?

num: ________

Step 8: Step through the remainder of the program.

Step 9: Remove the breakpoint.

Step 10: You can combine the pair of calculations that compute the user's age into one calculation. Replace these statements with the single statement

```
num = num / 3 - 8;
```

Step 11: Save the modified program as *guessage.cpp*.

Step 12: Compile, link, and run the modified program.

VERSION B: USE IF A DEBUGGER IS NOT AVAILABLE.

Step 1: Insert the statement

```
cout << "Input value of num:" << num;
```

after the statement

```
cin >> num;
```

Step 2: Insert the statement

```
cout << "After division:" << num;
```

after the statement

```
   num = num / 3;
```

Step 3: Run *guessage.cpp.*

Step 4: How does the value of num change?

```
Input value of num: ________
After division: ________
After subtraction: ________
```

Step 5: You can combine the pair of calculations that compute the user's age into one calculation. Replace these statements with the single statement

```
num = num / 3 - 8;
```

Step 6: Save the modified program as *guessage.cpp.*

Step 7: Compile, link, and run the modified program.

Laboratory 1: In-lab Exercise 2
SYNTACTIC AND LOGIC ERRORS

Date .... Section ....

Name ....

Natural languages such as English, Spanish, and Chinese have standard rules of usage for syntax and grammar. For example, the sentence

no money i got

violates several rules for standard English. Programming languages such as C++ also have standard rules describing how to write programs. If your code violates a C++ syntax rule, a message noting your **syntax error** is displayed when you attempt to compile your program. These types of mistakes are fairly easy to find when using a compiler that displays meaningful error messages.

A more subtle kind of error is a **semantic error,** or error in meaning. A statement with a semantic error is syntactically correct (legal) but functionally incorrect. For example, imagine that while on vacation in Australia you unexpectedly run into a friend from Spain whom you haven't seen in over 10 years. Upon seeing you, your Spanish friend says, "The world is a handkerchief!" At first, this response puzzles you, but then you realize that your friend has literally translated the expression "*El mundo es un pañuelo*" from Spanish. The sentence is syntactically correct, but the expression has no meaning in English. In programming, these semantic errors are called **logic errors**. A logic error occurs in your program when your code compiles without syntax errors but produces results that are not what you intended.

A DIAMOND IN THE ROUGH

The program in the file *carat.cpp* contains a syntax error and a logic error. You must first correct the syntax error so that the program compiles. Then you execute the "corrected" program and find the error in program logic.

Step 1: Attempt to compile the following program from the file *carat.cpp*.

```
// Converts the weight of a precious stone from carats to ounces.
// A carat is equal to 200 milligrams -- the approximate weight of
// one carob seed.

#include <iostream.h>

void main ()
{
    float caratWt,      // Weight of stone in carats
          milliWt,      // Weight of stone in milligrams
          gramWt,       // Weight of stone in grams
          ounceWt;      // Weight of stone in ounces

    // Prompt the user for the weight of a precious stone in carats.
    cout << endl            // What's missing?
    cout << "Enter a precious stone's weight (in carats): ";
    cin >> caratWt;

    // Compute the equivalent weight in ounces. One of the
    // calculations below is incorrect. Hint: Should the number of
    // grams be larger or smaller than the number of milligrams?

    // Convert from carats to milligrams.
    milliWt = caratWt * 200;
    cout << "This stone weighs " << milliWt << " milligrams." << endl;

    // Convert from milligrams to grams.
    gramWt = milliWt * 1000;
    cout << "This stone weighs " << gramWt << " grams." << endl;

    // Convert from grams to ounces.
    ounceWt = gramWt / 28.35;
    cout << "This stone weighs " << ounceWt << " ounces." << endl;
}
```

Step 2: What error message(s) does your compiler display?

Step 3: Correct the syntax error in the program.

Step 4: Save the revised program as *carat.cpp*.

Step 5: Compile, link, and run *carat.cpp*.

Step 6: Enter a value of 2 for the weight of a stone in carats.

Step 7: Write the output values the program displays in the spaces provided.

```
This stone weighs ___________ milligrams.

This stone weighs ___________ grams.

This stone weighs ___________ ounces.
```

Step 8: Determine whether or not the results are reasonable. *Hint*: Should the value for grams be larger than the value for milligrams?

Step 9: If you feel the results are not reasonable, check the weight conversion formulas and make any necessary adjustments.

Step 10: Save the revised program as *carat.cpp*.

Step 11: Compile, link, and run *carat.cpp*.

Step 12: Write the new output values your program produces for an input weight of 2 carats.

```
This stone weighs ___________ milligrams.

This stone weighs ___________ grams.

This stone weighs ___________ ounces.
```

Step 13: If the output still is not correct, make any necessary changes, and repeat steps 9 through 12.

Laboratory 1: Postlab Exercise

ERROR ANALYSIS

Date .... Section ....

Name ....

PART A

Suppose that you write a C++ program that generates several syntax errors when you compile it. How would you determine at what lines in the program the errors occur and what the errors are?

PART B

Suppose that your program compiles correctly—it does not contain any syntax errors—but it does not generate the expected results for certain test data. How would you determine where the errors in logic occur in the program and what the errors are?

C++ Program Elements

OVERVIEW

Laboratory 1 introduced you to the environment that you are using to create C++ programs. Now that you are familiar with your program development environment, you can examine more closely the language elements and program structure of C++ and construct your first C++ programs from scratch.

In the first Prelab Exercise, you create a program that prompts the user for a single input value, performs a simple calculation, and displays the results to the screen. The program that you develop in Prelab Exercise 2 requires multiple inputs and multiple outputs. You examine how to write meaningful prompts so that the user knows exactly what kind of input the program expects. The code that you create in the final Prelab Exercise requires a nonnumeric data type, `char`, to define variables that hold an alphanumeric character. You learn how to assign character values to variables, and you get more practice writing clear input prompts as part of a program that interactively creates a story.

Laboratory 2: Prelab Exercise 1

HOW PROGRAMS ARE ORGANIZED

Date .... Section ....

Name ....

BACKGROUND

What are the elements of a C++ program? Let's analyze the following program from the file *acreage.cpp*.

```
// Converts from square feet to acres.

#include <iostream.h>

void main()
{
    const float SQFEET_PER_ACRE = 43560.0;

    float sqFeet,    // Area in square feet
          acres;     // Area in acres

    // Prompt for area in square feet and read it in.
    cout << endl;
    cout << "Enter the area in square feet: ";
    cin >> sqFeet;

    // Calculate the acreage.
    acres = sqFeet / SQFEET_PER_ACRE;

    // Output the acreage.
    cout << "The acreage is " << acres << endl;
}
```

Any text on a line following a // is a comment and is ignored by the C++ compiler. For example, the line

```
// Converts from square feet to acres.
```

describes the purpose of *acreage.cpp*. Comments can appear on their own line or follow a C++ statement on the same line. The comment

```
// Area in square feet
```

describes the data that is stored in the floating-point variable `sqFeet`. **Comments** such as these explain to others (or remind you) what a program does and how it works. Collectively, the comments are referred to as the **program documentation**.

Almost all C++ programs contain at least one preprocessor directive. The line

```
#include <iostream.h>
```

instructs the compiler to include the declarations for the standard input/output stream header file *iostream.h.* The angle brackets tell the compiler to look for the iostream header file in the standard include directory—this directory contains all the standard header files for C++.

Every C++ program requires a `main()` function. You write the reserved word `void` before `main()` because no value is returned by the program to the operating system. You learn much more about how functions work in Laboratory 6, but for now use `void` with `main()` because some compilers give you a warning message if `main()` is used by itself.

Curly braces, { and }, are used to group statements. The left brace { shows where a **block** of statements begins, and the right brace } shows where the block ends. The braces following `void main()` in *acreage.cpp* show where the body of the program begins and ends.

The statements in the body of `main()` demonstrate several fundamental programming operations that you use in nearly all the C++ programs you create. These operations include describing (defining) the data to be used, collecting and storing the data, processing the data, and displaying the results.

You use identifiers to name the **variables** and constants your program needs. The declaration

```
float sqFeet,        // Area in square feet
      acres;         // Area in acres
```

tells the compiler to reserve locations in memory for two floating-point variables named `sqFeet` and `acres`, respectively. The semicolon ; signals the end of the declaration. The values assigned to these variables may change during the execution of a program. You use a **named constant** to represent a data value that will not be changed. The keyword `const` in the declaration

```
const float SQFEET_PER_ACRE = 43560.0;
```

tells the compiler that the floating-point variable `SQFEET_PER_ACRE` cannot change its value from `43560.0`. It is a convention in C++ to capitalize every letter in a named constant and to use underscores to separate the words in the identifier.

Input and output are handled using the input and output streams from the iostream library. The stream-insertion operator << is used with the standard output stream object `cout` to display information to the screen. For example, the statement

```
cout << "Enter the area in square feet: ";
```

outputs the string of characters enclosed by the double quotation marks to the screen.

Input is handled using the stream-extraction operator >> and the standard input stream object `cin`. When the computer executes the statement

```
cin >> sqFeet;
```

it takes the number you enter from the keyboard and stores it in the variable `sqFeet`.

The assignment statement

```
acres = sqFeet / SQFEET_PER_ACRE;
```

evaluates the expression `sqFeet / SQFEET_PER_ACRE` and assigns the result to the variable `acres`. The value of `acres` then is displayed to the screen by the statement

```
cout << "The acreage is " << acres << endl;
```

Note that this statement uses the << operator several times. The string in quotes is output first followed by the value of `acres`. The iostream manipulator `endl` is used to signal the end of the output line. The computer responds to `endl` by moving the cursor to the beginning of the next line on the screen.

WARM-UP EXERCISE

Complete the program below by filling in the missing comments and C++ code. A shell for this program is given in the file *cel2fahr.shl*.

```
// Converts a Celsius temperature to its Fahrenheit equivalent.

#include ____________   // Preprocessor directive for cin, cout, endl

void ___________
{
    float celsius,          // Celsius temperature reading
          fahrenheit __  ___________________________

    // Prompt for Celsius temperature and read it in.
    cout << endl << "Enter the Celsius temperature: ";
    cin >> celsius;

    // Calculate the equivalent Fahrenheit temperature.
    fahrenheit = 9.0 / 5.0 * celsius + 32;

    // __________________________________
    cout << "The Fahrenheit temperature is " << fahrenheit << endl;
____
```

THE RULE OF 72

You often hear someone on TV (especially between midnight and 4 A.M.) make the claim that by using their system you can double your investment in a few months or years. The "rule of 72" provides an easy way to compute how long it takes to double your money. The formula for this rule is

$$\textit{Years to double investment} = \frac{72}{\textit{interest rate}}$$

where *interest rate* (as a percent of 100) is the annual rate at which you earn interest on the investment. The rule assumes that interest is compounded annually and is not taxed.

Step 1: Create a program that computes the number of years it takes an investment to double using the rule of 72.

Input: Annual interest rate (as a percent of 100)

Output: Number of years it takes an investment to double

Step 2: Save your program as *ruleof72.cpp*.

Step 3: Complete the following test plan.

Test Plan for *ruleof72*			
Test case	*Sample data*	*Expected result*	*Checked*
High interest rate (12.5%)	12.5	5.76 years	
Medium interest rate (8%)	8.0		
Low interest rate (4%)			

```
/* This program computes the number of years
it takes for an investment to double */

~~float~~ #include <iostream>
void main ()
{
    float annIntRate;
    cout << "Enter the annual interest rate" endl;
    cin >> annIntRate;
    cout << endl;
    cout << "It will take" years " years endl;
    cout << for your money to double",
}
```

years = 72 / annIntRate

Laboratory 2: Prelab Exercise 2

INTERACTIVE INPUT AND OUTPUT

Date .... Section ....

Name ....

BACKGROUND

Most programs that you create require multiple input and output values. A common strategy for problems requiring multiple inputs is to individually prompt the user for each input value. For example, in a program requiring an employee's hours worked and hourly pay, you could write

```
cout << "Enter the hours worked: ";
cin >> hoursWorked;
cout << "Enter the pay rate: ";
cin >> payRate;
```

An alternative method is to request the inputs using a single prompt and a single `cin` statement. Multiple data items can be input by concatenating >> operators as in the following code segment:

```
cout << "Enter hours worked and pay rate separated by a space: ";
cin >> hoursWorked >> payRate;
```

WARM-UP EXERCISE

Complete the following program by filling in the missing C++ code. A shell for this program is given in the file *rectangl.shl.*

```
// Finds the perimeter and area of a rectangular field given its
// length and width in yards.

#include <iostream.h>

void main()
{
    float length,       // Length of field in yards
          width,        // Width of field in yards
          perimeter,    // Perimeter of field in yards
          area;         // Area of field in square yards
```

```
    // Insert your code below to prompt the user for the length
    // and width of a field and read in these values.




    // Calculate the perimeter and area of the field.
    perimeter = 2 * (length + width);
    area = length * width;

    // Output the calculated perimeter and area.
    cout << "The perimeter is " << perimeter << " yards." << endl;
    cout << ______________________________________________
}
```

ANY WAY YOU SLICE IT

When ordering pizza, people often argue about which size buys you the most pizza per dollar. A round pizza is usually identified by its diameter (10 inches, 12 inches, ...). You can compute its size in square inches using the formula for the area of a circle:

$$Size = \frac{\pi \cdot diameter^2}{4}$$

You then can calculate the pizza's price per square inch by dividing the price of the pizza by its size.

Step 1: Create a program that computes the size of a pizza and determines its price per square inch.

Input: Diameter of the pizza in inches
Price of the pizza in dollars and cents

Output: Size of the pizza in square inches
Price per square inch in dollars and cents

Step 2: Save your program as *pizzapi.cpp*.

Step 3: Complete the following test plan.

Test Plan for *pizzapi*			
Test case	*Sample data*	*Expected result*	*Checked*
Small pie 10-inch diameter Pizza price: $5.49	`10` `5.49`	Size of pizza: 78.54 square inches Price per square inch: $0.07	
Medium pie 12-inch diameter $6.99		Size of pizza: 113.10 square inches Price per square inch: $0.06	
Extra large pie 16-inch diameter $10			

Laboratory 2: Prelab Exercise 3

CHARACTER DATA

Date .... Section ....

Name ....

BACKGROUND

Modern programming languages include facilities to process text, as well as numerical data. C++ has a special data type, `char`, for dealing with alphanumeric characters. This section focuses on operations that you can use with individual characters. In Laboratory 7 you use arrays to manipulate groups of characters (strings).

You declare a variable that stores a single character value by writing `char` followed by the variable name. For example,

```
char firstInitial;
```

declares a variable that you might use to store a person's first initial.

You can assign a value to this variable using the assignment statement

```
firstInitial = 'J';
```

You must enclose the character `'J'` within single quotation marks to distinguish it from the variable name `J`. You can use the input stream object `cin` with the extraction operator >> to input character data. For example, you can write

```
cin >> firstInitial;
```

to read in a character from the keyboard and store it in the variable `firstInitial`. You do not enclose a character in single quotes when typing it in.

Three initials in succession can be read in using the statement

```
cin >> firstInitial >> middleInitial >> lastInitial;
```

If the user types in `JFK`, this statement stores `'J'` in `firstInitial`, `'F'` in `middleInitial`, and `'K'` in `lastInitial`. Spaces are ignored when inputting characters using the >> operator. Inputting

```
J F K
```

yields the same result as inputting

```
JFK
```

Laboratory 2: Bridge Exercise

TESTING AND DEBUGGING THE PRELAB APPLICATION EXERCISES

Date .... Section ....

Name ....

Check with your instructor whether you need to complete this exercise before your lab session or during lab.

THE RULE OF 72

Step 1: Execute your program in the file *ruleof72.cpp*.

Step 2: Check each case in your *ruleof72* test plan, and verify the expected result. If you discover mistakes in your program, correct them, and execute the test plan again.

ANY WAY YOU SLICE IT

Step 1: Execute your program in the file *pizzapi.cpp*.

Step 2: Check each case in your *pizzapi* test plan, and verify the expected result. If you discover mistakes in your program, correct them, and execute the test plan again.

A TALE TO TELL

Step 1: Execute your program in the file *story.cpp*.

Step 2: Check each case in your *story* test plan, and verify the expected result. If you discover mistakes in your program, correct them, and execute the test plan again.

Laboratory 2: In-lab Exercise 1

ARITHMETIC CALCULATIONS

Date 2-10-98 Section CS 131

Name Steve Lundback

BABY, IT'S COLD OUTSIDE

An important consideration when bundling up on a cold winter's day is the projected wind-chill factor. The wind-chill factor is the temperature without wind that has the same effect on exposed human skin as a given combination of wind and temperature—that is, the temperature you feel because of the wind. Wind-chill factor formulas can be derived for winds of various speeds. The wind-chill temperature for winds of 10, 25, and 40 miles per hour (mph) are listed below.

Wind-chill factor for a 10-*mph wind* = (1.23) *(actual temperature in °F)* –22
Wind-chill factor for a 25-*mph wind* = (1.48) *(actual temperature in °F)* –44
Wind-chill factor for a 40-*mph wind* = (1.58) *(actual temperature in °F)* –53

Note that these formulas assume that the temperature is in the range –45°F to 45°F.

Step 1: Create a program that computes the wind-chill factor for winds of 10, 25, and 40 miles per hour using the formulas listed above. The user inputs the actual temperature in degrees Fahrenheit, and the program outputs a table listing the wind-chill factors.

Input: Actual temperature (in degrees Fahrenheit)

Output: Table of wind-chill factors for winds of 10, 25, and 40 mph

Step 2: Save this program as *chilly.cpp*.

Step 3: Test your program using the following test plan. If you discover mistakes in your program, correct them, and execute the test plan again.

Data Types and Expressions

OVERVIEW

One of C++'s strong features is the number and utility of the operators it provides. In Laboratory 2 you used several of the arithmetic operators in formulas involving floating-point numbers. The formulas were simple and easily translated into C++ using the appropriate arithmetic operators (+, –, *, and /). Most programs that you create, however, require a careful consideration of the use of operators and how they work on different data types. In this lab, you learn programming techniques that give you more explicit control of operator precedence and data type conversions.

In Prelab Exercise 1, you examine the order in which C++ evaluates arithmetic operators. You experiment with changing the order in which operators are evaluated using parentheses. In Prelab Exercise 2, you use these same arithmetic operators with C++'s integer data type (`int`). In addition, you use the remainder operator, `%`, to perform modular arithmetic on integer values. In Prelab Exercise 3, you solve problems that require mixing floating-point and integer data types. You examine how and when the C++ compiler automatically converts an `int` value to a `float` value when these two data types are combined in a single expression. Finally, you learn a method for explicitly specifying when a data type conversion should be done.

Laboratory 3: Prelab Exercise 3

TYPE CONVERSION

Date .... Section ....

Name ....

BACKGROUND

You often will need to combine integer and floating-point values in the same expression. Whenever an integer value is combined with a floating-point value by an arithmetic operator, the integer value is automatically converted to floating-point form. This same conversion happens whenever an integer value is assigned to a floating-point variable. These implicit type conversions are referred to as **type coercions** or **type promotions**.

A more explicit way to convert data types is **type casting**. In this context, being typecast does not refer to the limited roles available to the cast of "Gilligan's Island" after syndication. Rather, a C++ cast operation consists of a type name and an expression enclosed in parentheses that will be converted to this type.

The following program from the file *typecast.cpp* uses a pair of casts to produce a floating-point result from the division of two integer variables. It produces this result by casting these variables to type `float` before the division is performed. These floating-point values then are used in evaluating the expression. Notice that this process does not change the type of variables `j` and `k` from `int` to `float`.

```
// Sample program using type casting for explicit type conversion.

#include <iostream.h>

void main()
{
    int j,k;
    cout << endl << "Enter two integers: ";
    cin >> j >> k;
    cout << "Integer division " << j / k << endl;
    cout << "Typecast float division " << float(j) / float(k);
}
```

Sample run:

```
Enter two integers: 2 5
Integer division 0
Typecast float division 0.4
```

WARM-UP EXERCISE

The formula to convert a Fahrenheit temperature to its Celsius equivalent is

$$C = \frac{5}{9}\,(F - 32)$$

Complete the following program by expressing the preceding formula in C++. A shell for this program is given in the file *fahr2cel.shl.*

```
// Converts a Fahrenheit temperature to its Celsius equivalent.

#include <iostream.h>

void main()
{
    float celsius,          // Celsius temperature reading
          fahrenheit;       // Fahrenheit temperature reading

    // Prompt for Fahrenheit temperature and read it in.
    cout << endl << "Enter a Fahrenheit temperature: ";
    cin >> fahrenheit;

    // Calculate the equivalent Celsius temperature.
    _______________________________________________________

    // Output the Celsius temperature.
    cout << "The equivalent Celsius temperature is " << celsius;
}
```

EXTRA BASES

One of the more interesting statistics for comparing power hitters in baseball is slugging percentage. A hitter's slugging percentage is calculated as follows:

$$\textit{Slugging percentage} = \frac{\textit{singles} + 2 \cdot \textit{doubles} + 3 \cdot \textit{triples} + 4 \cdot \textit{home runs}}{\textit{at-bats}}$$

Step 1: Create a program that determines a baseball player's slugging percentage using the preceding formula. Assume that all inputs are stored in variables of type `int`.

> *Input:* Number of singles, doubles, triples, home runs, and at-bats for a given player
>
> *Output:* The player's slugging percentage

Step 2: Save your program as *slugger.cpp.*

Step 3: Complete the following test plan.

Selection

OVERVIEW

Up to this point your programs have executed their statements in strict, sequential order from beginning to end. Most of your programs, however, will require control structures that allow the flow of execution to vary depending on the data input by the user (or read from a file). In this lab you use the if statement to specify alternate paths through a program.

In Prelab Exercise 1, you use relational operators to form conditional expressions—expressions that evaluate to either true or false. You then use these conditional expressions in conjunction with the if-else selection structure to choose a particular statement to execute from among a set of statements. In Prelab Exercise 2, you write a selection structure that executes a compound statement (a block of statements) if a particular condition is true. Finally, you use logical operators in Prelab Exercise 3 to test multiple conditions in a single conditional expression.

Laboratory 4: Prelab Exercise 1

IF-ELSE CONTROL STRUCTURES

Date .... Section ....

Name ....

BACKGROUND

Many times you only want to perform a particular action when a given condition is true. In C++, you use **relational operators** to express true/false relationships. C++'s relational operators and their meanings are listed below.

Operator	*Meaning*
>	Greater than
>=	Greater than or equal to
<	Less than
<=	Less than or equal to
==	Equal to
!=	Not equal to

A **conditional expression** is formed by combining a relational operator with a pair of values and/or variables. The resulting expression is either true or false. For example, the conditional expression

```
20 > 10
```

is true, while the conditional expression

```
18 == 15
```

is false. In C++, `1` represents true and `0` represents false. Thus the first expression yields the value `1`, and the second yields the value `0`.

The following program from the file *relops.cpp* performs three comparisons between the numeric value 20 and a number entered by the user.

```
// Comparing values using relational operators.

#include <iostream.h>

void main ()
{
    int number;
    cout << endl << "Number: ";
    cin >> number;
```

```
    cout << number << " > 20 is " << (number > 20) << endl;
    cout << number << " < 20 is " << (number < 20) << endl;
    cout << number << " == 20 is " << (number == 20) << endl;
}
```

The output of this program for the input value `10` is

```
Number: 10
10 > 20 is 0
10 < 20 is 1
10 == 20 is 0
```

The **if statement** is the simplest of C++'s selection structures. The if statement uses a conditional expression to determine whether a given statement should be executed. The following if statement

```
if ( temp>90 )
    cout << "Too hot" << endl;
```

outputs `"Too hot"` if `temp` is greater than 90—that is, if the conditional expression `temp>90` is true (yields the value `1`).

You can write a more general if statement by adding an else branch. In this case, one statement is executed if the conditional expression is true, and another statement is executed if it is not. An example of an **if-else statement** is

```
if ( temp>90 )
    cout << "Too hot" << endl;
else
    cout << "I feel good" << endl;
```

where `"Too hot"` is displayed if `temp` is greater than 90, and `"I feel good"` is displayed if it is not—that is, if `temp` is less than or equal to 90.

By nesting if-else statements, you can select from a set of alternatives, as in the following example:

```
if ( temp>90 )
    cout << "Too hot" << endl;
else
    if ( temp>32 )
        cout << "I feel good" << endl;
    else
        cout << "Too cold" << endl;
```

Suppose `temp` is 43. In this case, the first conditional expression is false. Thus the first else statement is executed, and `temp` is compared with 32. The second conditional expression is true, and the string `"I feel good"` is output. If `temp` is 25, however, both conditional expressions are false, and the string `"Too cold"` is output.

You can write this nested if-else structure in a form that is easier to read and interpret:

Loops

OVERVIEW

In Laboratory 4 you altered the sequential execution of a program using if statements to choose between alternate paths through the program. You need additional control structures, however, in order to repeat a statement multiple times. These control structures are called **loops**. In this lab you explore two types of loops: counter-controlled loops and event-controlled loops. A counter-controlled loop executes a predetermined number of times. An event-controlled loop executes until some event occurs that terminates the loop.

In Prelab Exercise 1, you use the for loop to create counter-controlled loops. You use while loops in Prelab Exercise 2 to develop event-controlled loops. In Prelab Exercise 3, you create loops that are both counter- and event-controlled.

LABORATORY 5: Cover Sheet

Date 3-10-98 Section CS 131

Name Steve Lundback

Place a checkmark in the *Assigned* column next to the exercises that your instructor has assigned to you. Have this sheet ready when your lab instructor checks your work. If your exercises are being checked outside the laboratory session, attach this sheet to the front of the packet of materials that you submit.

p. 85

Exercise		*Assigned*	*Completed*
Prelab 1	Counter-Controlled Loops		✓
Prelab 2	Event-Controlled Loops		
Prelab 3	Combined Counter/Event-Controlled Loops		
Bridge	Testing and Debugging the Prelab Application Exercises *Against All Odds* *Triskaidekaphobia* *You Auto Oil!*		
In-lab 1	Loops Containing Conditional Expressions		
In-lab 2	Nested Loops		
Postlab	Analyzing Loops		
		Total	

p. 8

Laboratory 5: Prelab Exercise 1

COUNTER-CONTROLLED LOOPS

Date 3-10-98 Section CS 131

Name Steve Lundback

BACKGROUND

A **for loop** executes a set of statements a fixed number of times. You typically use a for loop when you know in advance how many times you want to execute these statements. The following program from the file *for1.cpp* uses a for loop to control the size of a table of integers and their squares.

```
// Displays a table of integers and their squares.

#include <iostream.h>

void main()
{
    int j;    // Loop index

    // Display the headings for the table.
    cout << endl << "j" << "   Square" << endl;

    // Display the squares for the positive integers that are less
    // than or equal to five.
    for ( j = 1; j <= 5; j++ )
       cout << j << "      " << j * j << endl;
}
```

The for loop begins by initializing the loop control variable `j` to 1. It then evaluates the test expression `j<=5` for this value of `j`. The expression `1<=5` evaluates to true; thus the `cout` statement that forms the **loop body** is executed once, outputting a line containing 1 and its square (also 1). The expression `j++` completes the first pass through the loop by incrementing `j` by 1. A new pass begins by reevaluating the test expression `j<=5` for the new value of `j`. The test expression is still true, and the loop body is executed once again. This process is repeated until the value of `j` reaches 6. At this point, the test expression evaluates to false, and the loop terminates. The output produced by the program is shown below.

```
j      Square
1      1
2      4
3      9
4      16
5      25
```

You can change the program so that only odd positive integers are displayed by changing the increment expression.

```
for ( j = 1; j <= 5; j += 2 )
```

Note that the expression `j+=2` increments `j` by 2 each time the loop is executed.

You can use the decrement operator in a **`for`** statement to cause the loop control variable to "count down" from an initial value. The following program from the file *for2.cpp* uses a for loop to display a list of positive integers in descending order.

```
// "Counts down" to liftoff using a for loop.

#include <iostream.h>

void main()
{
    int j;          // Loop index
    int length;     // Length of countdown (in seconds)

    cout << endl << "Enter the length of the countdown (in secs): ";
    cin >> length;
    cout << "Countdown to liftoff: ";
    for ( j = length; j > 0; j-- )
        cout << j << " ";
    cout << endl << "***** Blast off! *****" << endl;
}
```

The expression `j--` decrements the value of `j` by 1 each time the loop is executed. Execution of the loop continues until the value of `j` is zero. A sample execution of the program is shown below.

```
Enter the length of the countdown (in seconds): 10
Countdown to liftoff: 10 9 8 7 6 5 4 3 2 1
***** Blast off! *****
```

WARM-UP EXERCISE

The **factorial** of a positive integer n is the product of the integers from 1 to n. Factorials are used commonly in probability and statistics to calculate the number of ways in which you can select elements from a set.

You can express the factorial of a positive integer n—written as $n!$—using the following formula:

$$n! = 1 \cdot 2 \cdot \ldots \cdot (n-2) \cdot (n-1) \cdot n$$

For example, 4! is $1 \cdot 2 \cdot 3 \cdot 4$.

Laboratory 5: Prelab Exercise 2

EVENT-CONTROLLED LOOPS

Date .... Section ....

Name ....

BACKGROUND

In an event-controlled loop, the number of times that the loop is executed is not predetermined. Instead, termination of the loop is triggered by the occurrence of some event. In the following program from the file *cubes.cpp*, for instance, the **while loop** terminates when the cube of an integer exceeds the value `MAX_CUBE`.

```
// Displays a table of positive integers and their cubes.

#include <iostream.h>

void main()
{
    const int MAX_CUBE = 99;
    int num = 1,
        numCubed = 1;

    cout << endl << "Number" << "Cube" << endl;

    // Execute the loop while numCubed does not exceed MAX_CUBE
    while ( numCubed <= MAX_CUBE )
    {
        cout << num << "        " << numCubed << endl;
        num++;
        numCubed = num * num * num;
    }
}
```

The while loop begins by checking whether `numCubed` is less than or equal to `MAX_CUBE`. The initial value of `numCubed` is 1—which is certainly less than `MAX_CUBE`—and the compound statement that forms the body of the loop is executed one time. The new value of `numCubed` is then compared with `MAX_CUBE`, and the loop is executed a second time. This process continues until the while condition becomes false—that is, until `numCubed` is greater than `MAX_CUBE`—at which point the loop terminates. The output produced by the program is shown below.

```
Number      Cube
1           1
2           8
3           27
4           64
```

When the conditions that terminate a loop's execution become complicated, you may want to use a Boolean flag to control the loop. You create a flag using an `int` variable in which you store one of two values: 0 (representing false) or 1 (representing true). The following program from the file *dataflag.cpp* uses a flag to indicate when the user has entered a number that is outside the range zero to one hundred.

```
//  Demonstrates the use of a Boolean flag.

#include <iostream.h>

void main()
{
    int validData = 1,      // Boolean flag, true (1) while data in range
        num,                // Input value
        count = 0;          // Number of input values
    float sum = 0.0;        // Sum of input values

    cout << endl;
    cout << "Enter numbers between 0 and 100 (out of range to stop):"
         << endl;

    // Loop until the input value is out of range.
    while ( validData )
    {
        cin >> num;
        if ( num >= 0   &&   num <= 100 )
        {
            sum += num;
            count++;
        }
        else
            validData = 0;
    }
    cout << "Average is " << sum / count << endl;
}
```

The `int` variable `validData` is initialized to 1 (true) in its declaration, which guarantees that the loop will be executed at least once. As long as the user enters data numbers between 0 and 100, the loop's conditional expression remains true, and the loop is executed. The flag `validData` is set to 0 when an out-of-range value is entered by the user. The loop's conditional expression then evaluates to false, and execution transfers to the statement following the loop. A sample run is shown below.

```
Enter numbers between 0 and 100 (out of range to stop):
50 95 77 -1
Average is 74
```

Step 3: Complete the following test plan.

Test Plan for *stones*			
Test case	*Sample data*	*Expected result*	*Checked*
Player 1 takes last stone	3 1 2 2 1 3 1	Player 1 wins!	
Player 2 takes last stone		Player 2 wins!	
Player 2 makes illegal selection	1 3 2 4 1 3 3		

Laboratory 5: Prelab Exercise 3

COMBINED COUNTER/EVENT-CONTROLLED LOOPS

Date .... Section ....

Name ....

BACKGROUND

The conditional expression controlling a loop often monitors both a counter and an event. In this case, loop execution continues either until the counter reaches some limit or until some event triggers loop termination. The following program from the file *words.cpp* includes an example of a combined counter/event-controlled loop.

```
// Echoes a sequence of characters until a ! is encountered or the
// number of characters output reaches MAX_COUNT.

#include <iostream.h>

const int MAX_COUNT = 10;

void main()
{
    char ch;
    int count = 0;    // Number of characters output

    cout << endl << "Enter a sequence of characters:" << endl;
    cin >> ch;
    while ( count < MAX_COUNT  &&  ch != '!' )
    {
         cout << ch;
         count++;
         cin >> ch;
    }
}
```

This loop terminates whenever the number of characters output reaches `MAX_COUNT`, as in the following example,

```
Enter a sequence of characters:
12345678901
1234567890
```

or whenever the character '!' is read in, as follows:

```
Enter a sequence of characters:
Flag! test
Flag
```

WARM-UP EXERCISE

The computer letter guessing game you developed in the last Warm-up Exercise never terminated if the user was unable to guess the letter—if the user kept guessing `'A'`, for example. In this exercise, you restrict the number of guesses the user can make.

Complete the following program by filling in the missing C++ code. A shell for this program is given in the file *gueslet3.shl.*

```
#include<iostream.h>

void main()
{
    const char COMP_LET = 'M';     // Letter chosen by computer
    const int MAX_GUESSES = 5;     // Max guesses allowed

    int numGuesses = _____,        // Count of player guesses
        guessed = _____;           // Boolean flag for game over
    char playerGuess;              // Player guess

    cout << endl << "I am thinking of a CAPITAL letter...";

    // Loop until the user guesses the correct letter or the number of
    // guesses reaches the maximum number allowed.
    while ( ______________________________________________ )
    {
        cout << "What is your guess? ";
        cin >> playerGuess;
        numGuesses++;
        if ( playerGuess > COMP_LET )
            cout << "Your guess is too high" << endl;
        else if ( playerGuess < COMP_LET )
            cout << "Your guess is too low" << endl;
        else
            guessed = __;
    }

    // Check if letter was correctly guessed.
    if ( ___________ )
       cout << "Congratulations, you guessed my letter in "
            << numGuesses << " guess(es)";
    else
       cout << "Sorry, you lose. The letter was " << COMP_LET << ".";
    cout << endl;
}
```

YOU AUTO OIL!

Automobile mechanics recommend that you change your car's oil every 3 months (13 weeks) or when you have driven 3000 miles since your last oil change. In this exercise you create a program that determines when an oil change is needed and tells the user why he or she needs the oil change based on the 3 months/3000 miles guideline.

Step 1: Create a program that determines when an oil change is needed. Your program should begin by prompting for the odometer reading at the last oil change and then prompt for a series of week-by-week odometer readings. This process should continue until your program detects that an oil change is needed based on the 13 week/3000 miles standard, at which point the process should terminate and an explanation of why the oil change is needed should be displayed.

Input: Odometer reading at last oil change
Week-by-week odometer readings

Output: A message explaining why the oil change is required

Step 2: Save your program as *oilauto.cpp*.

Step 3: Complete the following test plan.

Test Plan for *oilauto*			
Test case	*Sample data*	*Expected result*	*Checked*

Car driven at least 3000 miles since last oil change	`15000`
	`15500`
	`16500`
	`17750`
	`18250`
		Oil change required—you have driven 3250 miles since your last oil change	

Three months have passed since last oil change			

Laboratory 5: Bridge Exercise

TESTING AND DEBUGGING THE PRELAB APPLICATION EXERCISES

Date .... Section ....

Name ....

Check with your instructor whether you need to complete this exercise before your lab session or during lab.

AGAINST ALL ODDS

Step 1: Execute your program in the file *odds.cpp*.

Step 2: Check each case in your *odds* test plan, and verify the expected result. If you discover mistakes in your program, correct them, and execute the test plan again.

TRISKAIDEKAPHOBIA

Step 1: Execute your program in the file *stones.cpp*.

Step 2: Check each case in your *stones* test plan, and verify the expected result. If you discover mistakes in your program, correct them, and execute the test plan again.

YOU AUTO OIL!

Step 1: Execute your program in the file *oilauto.cpp*.

Step 2: Check each case in your *oilauto* test plan, and verify the expected result. If you discover mistakes in your program, correct them, and execute the test plan again.

Laboratory 5: In-lab Exercise 1

LOOPS CONTAINING CONDITIONAL EXPRESSIONS

Date .... Section ....

Name ....

KEY COMBINATION

You often have to enter a secret code or password to gain entrance to a restricted area or to gain access to a computer network. In many cases the password consists of a sequence of alphanumeric characters that must be entered in a specified order. In this exercise you create a program that "opens the door" to a restricted area when the user enters the correct two-character sequence.

Step 1: Create a program that reads in characters until the user enters the correct two-character sequence (`cs`) to open the door. A shell for this program is given in the file *opendoor.shl.*

Input: A sequence of characters

Output: A message informing the user that the door is now open

Step 2: Save your program as *opendoor.cpp.*

Step 3: Test your program using the following test plan. If you discover mistakes in your program, correct them, and execute the test plan again.

Test Plan for *opendoor*

Test case	*Sample data*	*Expected result*	*Checked*
Legal entrance	`cs`	Door opens	
Hacker	`imacsmajor`	Door opens	
Two c's followed by an s	`ccs`	Door opens	

Laboratory 5: In-lab Exercise 2

NESTED LOOPS

Date .... Section ....

Name ....

HOT ENOUGH FOR YA?

People who are originally from cities such as New York and St. Louis and who have moved to states such as Arizona and New Mexico often say that despite higher temperatures in these southwestern states, they experience less discomfort than they did in their place of origin. This discomfort is due in large part to the high rate of relative humidity in such cities as New York and St. Louis during the summer. A method for measuring the discomfort caused by humidity is the temperature-humidity index (THI). The formula for computing the THI is

$$THI = temperature - 0.0055(100 - relative\ humidity)(temperature - 58)$$

where *temperature* is measured in degrees Fahrenheit and *relative humidity* is measured as a percentage of 100. Most people feel uncomfortable when the THI is 80 or above, and readings in the 90s are considered quite dangerous. A table listing THI values for sample temperatures and humidity levels is shown below.

	Humidity		
Temp	**80**	**90**	**100**
80	77.58	78.79	80.00
90	86.48	88.24	90.00
100	95.38	97.69	100.00

Step 1: Create a program that displays a THI table in which the relative humidity ranges from 40% to 100% and the temperature ranges from 60°F to 100°F. Use an increment of 10 along each row and column.

Input: None

Output: THI table

Step 2: Save your program as *thi.cpp*.

Step 3: Test your program using the following test plan. If you discover mistakes in your program, correct them, and execute the test plan again.

Test Plan for *thi*			
Test case	*Sample data*	*Expected result*	*Checked*
Low temp Low humidity	60 50	THI of 59.45	
High temp Low humidity	100 40	THI of 86.14	
High temp High humidity	100 90	THI of 97.69	

Laboratory 5: Postlab Exercise

ANALYZING LOOPS

Date .... Section ....

Name ....

PART A

A common programming error is to create a loop that loops one too many or one too few times. This kind of logic error is referred to as an **"off by one" error**. The following program from the file *loopy.cpp* calculates an incorrect average for most data sets because of an "off by one" error.

```
// Loop suffers from an "off by one" error.

#include <iostream.h>

void main ()
{
    int num,
        count = 1;
    float sum = 0.0;

    cout << endl;
    while ( count <= 3 )
    {
        cout << "Enter a number: ";
        cin >> num;
        sum += num;
        count++;
    }
    cout << "Average is " << sum / count << endl;
}
```

Describe the program's "off by one" logic error, and modify the program so that the correct average is calculated.

PART B

Another common programming error is to create a loop that never terminates. The resulting loop is referred to as an **infinite loop**. The following program from the file *forever.cpp* is designed to display 10 rows of 5 stars but instead displays stars forever. Explain why the nested loops never terminate, and correct the program.

```
// Fix the infinite loop.

#include <iostream.h>

void main ()
{
    int j;
    for ( j = 0; j < 10; j++ )
    {
        for ( j = 0; j < 5; j++ )
            cout << '*';
        cout << endl;
    }
}
```

Functions

OVERVIEW

Ask a C aficionado to define a program, and she or he is likely to respond, "A program is a collection of functions." Ask the same question of a C++ programmer, and you are likely to hear, "A program is a collection of interacting objects that contain functions." In this lab you lay the groundwork for a modular (or structured) approach to programming in which you divide the tasks your programs must perform among several functions. In later labs you extend this modular approach into an object-oriented programming style based on the use of classes and objects.

The programs you wrote in previous labs were relatively short, consisting of a single function—`main()`. Most applications, however, yield programs that are comprised of many functions, each playing a different role within a program. This division of a complex task into simpler subtasks makes it easier for you to design, debug, and maintain programs. Moreover, the functions you create for one program are likely to be reused in later programs, further shortening the time it takes to develop a program.

In Prelab Exercise 1, you experiment with a set of standard C++ library functions. In Prelab Exercise 2, you begin creating your own functions. Prelab Exercise 3 focuses on the development of void functions—functions that perform a task without returning a value.

LABORATORY 6: Cover Sheet

Date .... Section ....

Name ....

Place a checkmark in the *Assigned* column next to the exercises that your instructor has assigned to you. Have this sheet ready when your lab instructor checks your work. If your exercises are being checked outside the laboratory session, attach this sheet to the front of the packet of materials that you submit.

Exercise		*Assigned*	*Completed*
Prelab 1	Library Functions		
Prelab 2	Creating Functions		
Prelab 3	Void Functions		
Bridge	Testing and Debugging the Prelab Application Exercises *Ancient Secrets* *Low, Low Monthly Payments* *Getting Out of Hock*		
In-lab 1	Calling Functions in Loops		
In-lab 2	Applying Functions that Return a Value		
Postlab	Scope and Visibility		
		Total	

Laboratory 6: Prelab Exercise 1

LIBRARY FUNCTIONS

Date .... Section ....

Name ....

BACKGROUND

A **function** is a named piece of code that performs a well-defined task. As your experience with programming increases, you begin to notice that you do certain tasks over and over again. Some tasks are so common—finding a square root, testing whether an alphanumeric character is a letter, generating a random number, and getting the current time, to name a few—that standard functions have been developed to perform these tasks. Functions that relate in some thematic sense are collected together into standard **function libraries**.

C++'s math library, for instance, contains an extensive collection of mathematical functions. The following program from the file *sqroot.cpp* uses one of these functions, `sqrt()`, to calculate the square root of a number.

```
//  Calculates the square root of a number using the sqrt() function.

#include <iostream.h>
#include <math.h>    // Include prototype for sqrt()

void main()
{
   double num;    // Number whose square root is computed

   // Prompt the user for a number and read it in.
   cout << endl << "Enter a number: ";
   cin >> num;

   // Display the square root of the number.
   cout << "Square root is " << sqrt(num) << endl;
}
```

The expression `sqrt(num)` is referred to as a **call** to function `sqrt()`. This call consists of two parts: the **name** of the function, `sqrt`, and the **argument** whose value is passed to the function, `num`. Note that the argument is placed inside parentheses following the function name—a notational style borrowed from mathematics. When called, the `sqrt()` function takes the value of argument `num` and returns its square root.

Whenever you use a library function, you must include the header file for the library in your program. The preprocessor directive

```
#include <math.h>
```

for example, includes the header file for the standard math library. The header file for a library contains the prototypes for the functions in the library. Each **prototype** specifies the name of a function, the type of data returned by the function, and a list of function **parameters** that includes the data type of each parameter. A prototype for the `sqrt()` function from *math.h* is shown below.

```
double sqrt( double x );
```

This prototype indicates that the `sqrt()` function returns a value of type `double` and has one parameter, which also is of type `double`. The parameter name `x` given in the prototype is for informational purposes only and does not necessarily match the name of the argument used in a call to the function—the argument `num` in the call `sqrt(num)`, for instance.

WARM-UP EXERCISE

The power function computes the value of x^y—that is, x raised to the power y. The *math.h* header file includes the following prototype for the C++ power function, `pow()`:

```
double pow( double x, double y );
```

The following program uses this function to raise a number to a power, where both the number and the power are input by the user. Complete this program by filling in the missing C++ code. A shell for this program is given in the file *power.shl*.

```
//  Computes the value of a number raised to a power.

#include <iostream.h>
______________________          // Header file for pow()

void main()
{
    double number,          // Number whose power is to be computed
           exponent;        // Power to which number is raised

    // Prompt the user to enter a number and an exponent and read in
    // these values.
    cout << endl << "Input the number: ";
    cin >> number;
    cout << "Input the power: ";
    cin >> exponent;

    // Insert code that computes number raised to the exponent power and
    // displays the result.
```

ANCIENT SECRETS

Carbon-14 is a naturally occurring radioactive carbon isotope. A living plant contains the same proportion of carbon-14 as the atmosphere in which the plant is grown. When the plant dies, its carbon-14 gradually undergoes radioactive decay. The rate of decay is exponential, with half the carbon-14 decaying approximately every 5700 years.

If you have an artifact containing plant material—wood or cloth, for instance—you can compute the approximate age of the artifact from the amount of carbon-14 remaining in a sample of the plant material using the following formula:

$$Age = -5700 \cdot \frac{ln\ (percentage\ of\ carbon\text{–}14\ remaining)}{ln\ (2)}$$

where *age* is the approximate age of the artifact (in years), *percentage of carbon-14 remaining* is the percentage of carbon-14 remaining in the sample (as a fraction of 1.0), and *ln* is the natural (Napierian) logarithm.

Step 1: Create a program that computes the age of an artifact using the carbon-14 dating formula above.

Input: Percentage of carbon-14 remaining in a sample of plant material from the artifact (as a fraction of 1.0)

Output: The approximate age of the artifact

Step 2: Save your program as *carbon.cpp*.

Step 3: Complete the following test plan.

Test Plan for *carbon*

Test case	*Sample data*	*Expected result*	*Checked*
20% carbon-14 remaining in sample	`0.2`	Artifact approximately 13,235 years old	
50% carbon-14 remaining in sample			

Laboratory 6: Prelab Exercise 2

CREATING FUNCTIONS

Date .... Section ....

Name ....

BACKGROUND

In addition to providing a rich set of predefined functions, C++ gives you the ability to create your own functions as well. The `sumSequence()` function in the file *sumseq.cpp* computes the sum of a sequence of integers.

```
// Displays the sum of the integers from 1 to a number entered by the
// user.

#include <iostream.h>

int sumSequence ( int n );    // Function prototype

void main()
{
    int num;   // Final term of sequence

    cout << endl << "Enter the final term of the sequence: ";
    cin >> num;

    // Display the sum.
    cout << "The sum of the integers from 1 to " << num << " is "
         << sumSequence(num) << endl;
}

// Function implementation

int sumSequence ( int n )
// Returns the sum of the integers from 1 to n.
{
    int sum = 0;    // Stores sum
    for (int j = 1; j <= n; j++)
        sum += j;
    return sum;
}
```

Let's examine the mechanics of creating a function. You begin by creating a function prototype. The prototype for `sumSequence()` is shown below:

```
int sumSequence( int n );
```

This prototype informs the compiler that the `sumSequence()` function has a single-integer argument and returns an integer value. Note that this prototype must appear before any call to the `sumSequence()` function.

The function prototype is used by the compiler when processing the call

```
sumSequence(num)
```

When this call is made, `sumSequence()` will receive (as input) a copy of the current value of variable `num` via parameter `n`. The compiler checks that the number of arguments and their respective data types are the same in both the function call and the function prototype's parameter list. Note that the name of the argument in the function call (`num`) is different from the name of the parameter in the function prototype (`n`)—they can have the same name but usually their names are different.

By convention, the implementation of the `sumSequence()` function is placed after `main()`. The function declaration is repeated—note that this time there is no semicolon at the end. The statements in the **function body** use the value of parameter `n` to compute the sum of the sequence of integers from one to `n`. This sum is returned to the calling function—in this example the function `main()`—by the statement

```
return sum;
```

The variable `sum` in function `sumSequence()` stores the sum as it is calculated. Variables like `sum` that are declared within a function are referred to as **local variables**. Local variables can only be used within the function in which they are defined. You could not use `sum` in `main()`, for example. You examine the scope of local variables in the Postlab Exercise.

WARM-UP EXERCISE

A function prototype provides the compiler with the information it needs in order to compile calls to the function. In order for us to understand what the function does, we often need more information about the function's parameters and the value returned by the function. We will present this information using a **function specification** in which the function prototype is supplemented with text descriptions of parameters, returned values, and so forth.

The following specification describes a function that computes factorials:

`long factorial ( int n )`

Input parameter

`n:` the number whose factorial is to be computed

Returns

The factorial of **n**

Complete the following program by filling in the missing C++ code. A shell for this program is given in the file *factfunc.shl*.

```
// Computes n!

#include <iostream.h>

long factorial ( int n );    // Function prototype (declaration)

void main()
{
    int num;    // Number whose factorial is to be computed

    cout << endl << "Input the number: ";
    cin >> num;

    // Display the factorial of the number.
    cout << num << "! is " << ____________________ << endl;
}

// Implementation of factorial()

______________________________     // Function return type, name and
                                   // parameters
{
    long fact = 1;    // Stores factorial
    for ( int j = 1; j <= n; j++ )
        fact *= j;
    return _________;
}
```

Low, Low Monthly Payments

You can compute the monthly payment on a fully amortized loan if you know the amount borrowed (principal), the annual interest rate, and the length of the loan. The following formula computes a monthly loan payment where *mpr* is the monthly percentage (interest) rate and *numMonths* is the length of the loan in months:

$$Monthly\ Payment = mpr \cdot \frac{principal}{1 - \dfrac{1}{(1 + mpr)^{numMonths}}}$$

Step 1: Create a function `monthlyPayment()` that computes the monthly payment on a fully amortized loan. Base your function on the following specification:

```
double monthlyPayment ( double principal, double annualRate,
                        int numYears                        )
```

Input parameters
`principal:` amount borrowed (in dollars)
`annualRate:` annual interest rate (as a percentage of 1.0)
`numYears:` length of the loan (in years)
Returns
The monthly payment (in dollars and cents)

Note that the monthly percentage rate is one-twelfth the annual interest rate.

Step 2: Add your `monthlyPayment()` function to the test program *testpay.cpp*.

Step 3: Complete the following test plan.

Test Plan for *monthlyPayment()*			
Test case	*Sample data*	*Expected result*	*Checked*

$1000 borrowed
10% interest
1 year
	`1000`
	`0.1`
	`1`
		Monthly payment: $87.92	

$5000 borrowed
5% interest
2 years
	`5000`
	`0.05`
	`2`
		Monthly payment: $219.36	

$10,000 borrowed 8.9% interest 10 years		Monthly payment: $126.14	

Laboratory 6: Prelab Exercise 3

VOID FUNCTIONS

Date .... Section ....

Name ....

BACKGROUND

Some functions perform tasks that do not result in a value being returned to the calling routine. Such functions are referred to as **void functions**. One example of a void function is a routine that displays information. The void function `lineOfChars()` from the file *linechar.cpp* displays a line by outputting a specified character a number of times.

```
// Demonstrates the use of a void function to display a line of
// characters.

#include <iostream.h>

void lineOfChars ( char lineChar, int size );    // Function prototype

void main()
{
    char lineChar;      // Character used to form line
    int lineLength;     // Length of line

    // Display a line of 30 asterisks.
    lineOfChars('*', 30);

    cout << "Enter character and length: ";
    cin >> lineChar >> lineLength;

    // Display the line of characters specified by the user.
    lineOfChars(lineChar,lineLength);
}

// Implementation of lineOfChars()
void lineOfChars ( char lineChar, int size )

// Displays a line by displaying lineChar size times.
{
    int j;
    for ( j = 0; j < size; j++ )
        cout << lineChar;
    cout << endl;
}
```

Two calls are made to `lineOfChars()`. In the first call,

```
lineOfChars('*', 30);
```

the character constant `'*'` and the integer constant `30` are passed to `lineOfChars()`, and the function displays a line containing 30 asterisks. In the second call,

```
lineOfChars(lineChar,lineLength);
```

the values of the variables `lineChar` and `lineLength` are passed to function `lineOfChars()`. Note that because `lineOfChars()` does not return a value, the calls to `lineOfChars()` are statements by themselves. A sample execution of the program is shown below:

```
******************************
Enter character and length: = 27
===========================
```

WARM-UP EXERCISE

Void functions are commonly used to output information. The following function displays a table showing how an investment grows over time:

```
void investmentTable ( double principal,
                       double interestRate,
                       int timePeriod      );
```

Input parameters
`principal:` amount invested (in dollars)
`interestRate:` annual interest rate (as a percentage of 1.0)
`timePeriod:` length of the investment (in years)

Outputs
A table showing the following for each year of the investment: the amount of interest earned during that year and the value of the investment at the end of the year. Assumes that interest is compounded annually.

Complete the following program by filling in the missing C++ code. A shell for this program is given in the file *invest.shl*.

```
// Displays a table showing yearly interest earned on an investment
// and the updated value. Assumes that interest is compounded annually.

#include <iostream.h>
#include <iomanip.h>

// investmentTable() prototype
void investmentTable( double principal,
                      double interestRate,
                      int timePeriod      );
```

```
void main ()
{
    double amtInvested,     // Original investment (in dollars)
           intRate;         // Annual interest rate (as a % of 1.0)
    int numYears;           // Length of the investment (in years)

    // Prompt the user and read in the amount invested, the interest rate,
    // and the duration of the investment.
    cout << endl << "Enter the amount invested: ";
    cin >> amtInvested;
    cout << "Enter the annual interest rate (as a % of 1.0): ";
    cin >> intRate;
    cout << "Enter the length of the investment (in years): ";
    cin >> numYears;

    // Display table.
    investmentTable(_______, _______, _______);
}


//--------------------------------------------------------------------

void investmentTable( double principal,
                      double interestRate,
                      int timePeriod       )

// Displays a table showing interest earned each year and the value of the
// investment.

{
    double interestEarned,    // Yearly interest earned
           value;             // Investment plus interest earned

    // Display the investment table.
    cout << endl;
    cout << "  Year     Interest Earned     Updated Value " << endl;
    cout << "  ----     ---------------     ------------- " << endl;

    // Set output formatting for floating-point values to display
    // two digits of precision to the right of the decimal point.
    cout << setprecision(2) << setiosflags(ios::fixed|ios::showpoint);

    // Set the value equal to the initial investment.
    value = principal;

    // Display yearly accumulated interest and updated value.
    for ( int j = 1; j <= timePeriod; j++ )
    {
        interestEarned = ____________________________;
        value += ____________________;
        cout << setw(6) << j
             << setw(20) << interestEarned
             << setw(18) << value << endl;
    }
}
```

GETTING OUT OF HOCK

Part of each payment on a loan goes toward paying off the interest, and part goes toward paying off the principal. With a typical amortized loan, you pay much more toward interest at the start of the loan period and much more toward principal at the end. The following formulas compute the amount you pay in interest and principal for a given month:

$$\text{Interest paid} = mpr \cdot balance$$
$$\text{Principal paid} = \text{monthly payment} - \text{interest paid}$$

where *mpr* is the monthly percentage (interest) rate, *balance* is the balance due on the loan at the start of the month, and *monthly payment* is the monthly payment on the loan.

A loan schedule is a table showing the interest paid, principal paid, and balance remaining for each month in the life of a loan. An outline of a sample loan schedule is shown below:

Amount borrowed = $1000
Annual interest rate as a percentage of 1.0 = 0.1
Length of loan = 1 year
Monthly payment = $87.92

Month	*Interest Paid*	*Principal Paid*	*Remaining Balance*
1	8.33	79.58	920.42
2	7.67	80.25	840.17
.	.	.	.
.	.	.	.
12	0.73	87.19	0.00

Step 1: Create a function `loanSchedule()` that displays a loan schedule for a fully amortized loan. Base your function on the following specification:

```
void loanSchedule ( double principal, double annualRate,
                    int numYears                          )
```

Input parameters
`principal`: amount borrowed (in dollars)
`annualRate`: annual interest rate (as a percentage of 1.0)
`numYears`: length of the loan (in years)

Outputs
A loan schedule for a fully amortized loan.

Note that the `monthlyPayment()` function you created in Prelab Exercise 2 computes the monthly payment on a fully amortized loan.

Step 2: Add your `loanSchedule()` function to the file *testloan.cpp*.

Step 3: Complete the following test plan.

Test Plan for *loanSchedule()*			
Test case	*Sample data*	*Expected result*	*Checked*

$5000 borrowed
5% interest
2 years
	`5000`
	`0.05`
	`2`
		Monthly payment: $219.36
		
		Month / Interest Paid / Principal Paid / Remaining Balance
		1 / 20.83 / 198.52 / 4801.48
		2 / 20.01 / 199.35 / 4602.13
		. / . / . / .
		. / . / . / .
		24 / 0.91 / 218.45 / 0.00	

$100,000 borrowed
7.9% interest
20 years
	`100000`
	`0.079`
	`20`
		Monthly payment: $830.23
		
		Month / Interest Paid / Principal Paid / Remaining Balance
		1 / 658.33 / 171.89 / 99828.11
		2 / 657.20 / 173.03 / 99655.08
		. / . / . / .
		. / . / . / .
		240 / 5.43 / 824.80 / 0.00	

$1000 borrowed 15% interest 1 year			

Laboratory 6: Bridge Exercise

TESTING AND DEBUGGING THE PRELAB APPLICATION EXERCISES

Date .... Section ....

Name ....

Check with your instructor whether you need to complete this exercise before your lab session or during lab.

ANCIENT SECRETS

Step 1: Execute your program in the file *carbon.cpp*.

Step 2: Check each case in your *carbon* test plan, and verify the expected result. If you discover mistakes in your program, correct them, and execute the test plan again.

LOW, LOW MONTHLY PAYMENTS

Step 1: Execute the program in the file *testpay.cpp*.

Step 2: Check each case in your *monthlyPayment()* test plan, and verify the expected result. If you discover mistakes in your function, correct them, and execute the test plan again.

GETTING OUT OF HOCK

Step 1: Execute the program in the file *testloan.cpp*.

Step 2: Check each case in your *loanSchedule()* test plan, and verify the expected result. If you discover mistakes in your function, correct them, and execute the test plan again.

Laboratory 6: In-lab Exercise 1

CALLING FUNCTIONS IN LOOPS

Date .... Section ....

Name ....

TRISKAIDEKAPHOBIA REVISITED

In this exercise you add "functionality" to the "Thirteen Stones" program you developed in Laboratory 5, Prelab Application Exercise 2. In the new version of the game, your program replaces one of the players (Player 1), and the remaining human player competes against your program. Rather than asking Player 1 to enter a move, your program calls the following function to determine Player 1's move:

`int player1Pick ( int numStones, int player2Pick )`

Input parameters

`numStones`: number of stones remaining

`player2Pick`: number of stones Player 2 took on her or his last move (if any)

Returns

The number of stones (1, 2, or 3) that Player 1 wishes to pick up.

Having your program take the place of Player 1 is no coincidence. It turns out that because Player 1 goes first your program will always win if it picks the correct number of stones on each move. See if you can determine Player 1's strategy from the following sample game:

```
Number of stones remaining: 13
Player 1's pick: 1
Number of stones remaining: 12
Player 2's pick: 1
Number of stones remaining: 11
Player 1's pick: 3
Number of stones remaining: 8
Player 2's pick: 2
Number of stones remaining: 6
Player 1's pick: 2
Number of stones remaining: 4
Player 2's pick: 3
Number of stones remaining: 1
Player 1's pick: 1
The winner is Player 1!
```

If you noticed that Player 1 took one stone on the first move and (4 – Player 2's last pick) stones on each subsequent move, then you are very clever indeed!

Step 1: Create the function `player1Pick()` specified above. Your function should ensure a victory by Player 1 by using the optimal selection strategy outlined above.

Step 2: Modify your *stones.cpp* program from Laboratory 5 so that the program takes the place of Player 1. Use your `player1Pick()` function to generate Player 1's moves. Save the new version of your program as *slystone.cpp*.

Step 3: Test your program using the following test plan. If you discover mistakes in your program, correct them and execute the test plan again.

Test Plan for *slystone*			
Test case	*Sample data*	*Expected result*	*Checked*
Player 1 selects last stone	1 3 1 2 2 3 1	Player 1 wins!	
Player 1 selects last stone Includes illegal move by player 2	1 1 3 2 2 4 2 2	Player 1 wins!	

Laboratory 6: In-lab Exercise 2

APPLYING FUNCTIONS THAT RETURN A VALUE

Date .... Section ....

Name ....

PYRAMID POWER

In the famous Apex card trick, a magician gives a volunteer from the audience four decks of cards from which all the tens and face cards have been removed. The volunteer selects any five cards and places them face up in a row. The magician then chooses one of the cards remaining in the deck and places it behind the volunteer's left ear.

At this point, the volunteer begins building a pyramid of cards from bottom to top by applying the following rule to each pair of adjacent cards in each row in the pyramid:

Add the rank of the cards. If the sum is greater than 9, then add the digits in the sum. Select a card whose rank is the sum computed above and place this card above the pair of cards.

The following pyramid is built from the cards 8, 6, 4, 5, and 2:

```
    6
   7 8
  6 1 7
 5 1 9 7
8 6 4 5 2
```

Adding cards 8 and 6, for example, yields the sum 14. Adding the digits of this sum—1 and 4—produces 5, and a 5 is placed above cards 8 and 6. Similarly, cards 4 and 5 sum to 9, so a 9 is placed above 4 and 5.

Once the pyramid is complete, the magician takes the card from behind the volunteer's ear, and suprisingly enough, it is a 6, precisely the card at the apex of the pyramid. How did the magician know which card to select? The trick is to use the following rules derived from Pascal's triangle:

$$x = \textit{the remainder of} \left(\frac{card1 + 4 \cdot card2 + 6 \cdot card3 + 4 \cdot card4 + card5}{9} \right)$$

If x equals zero, then the apex card is 9. Otherwise, the apex card is x.

where the cards on the bottom row are numbered from left to right.

Step 1: Create a function `apex()` that returns the rank (1–9) of the card at the apex of the pyramid. Base your function on the following specification:

```
int apex ( int card1, int card2, int card3, int card4, int card5 )
```

Input parameters

card1, card2, card3, card4, card5: bottom row of cards from left to right

Returns

The rank (1–9) of the card at the apex of the pyramid

Step 2: Add your `apex()` function to the file *testapex.cpp*.

Step 3: Test your function using the following test plan. If you discover mistakes in your function, correct them, and execute the test plan again.

Test Plan for *apex()*			
Test case	*Sample data*	*Expected result*	*Checked*
Lucky seven	4 1 7 9 2	Apex card: 7	
All nines	9 9 9 9 9	Apex card: 9	
Your data		Apex card: 1	

Laboratory 6: Postlab Exercise

SCOPE AND VISIBILITY

Date .... Section ....

Name ....

PART A

The following program from the file *fun1.cpp*

```
#include <iostream.h>

void foo();

void main()
{
    int j = 5;
    cout << endl << "j in main() is " << j << endl;
    foo();
    cout << "j in main() is " << j << endl;
}

void foo()
{
    int j = 10;
    cout << "j in foo() is " << j << endl;
}
```

produces the output shown below:

```
j in main() is 5
j in foo() is 10
j in main() is 5
```

Explain why the value displayed for `j` in `main()` is `5` and the value displayed for `j` in `foo()` is `10`.

PART B

- The following program from the file *fun2.cpp*

```
#include <iostream.h>

int square ();

void main()
{
    int k = 5;
    cout << endl << k << " squared is " << square() << endl;
}

int square ()
{
    return k * k;
}
```

does not compile. Why not? What would you do to fix the program?

Arrays

OVERVIEW

Most of the data we encounter in everyday life occur in groups rather than in individual pieces. We tend to collect these related data items into conceptual units to which we assign names—a group of birds is a flock, a collection of students is a class, and so forth. In C++, arrays are used to store groups of similar items in a named collection. What makes arrays particularly useful is the ease and efficiency with which you can access individual items, particularly when all (or some) of the items in the array are accessed as part of an iterative process—when finding the largest bird in a flock, for instance.

In Prelab Exercise 1, you examine how to declare an array and how to reference individual array elements. You learn how to pass arrays to functions in Prelab Exercise 2. In Prelab Exercise 3, you examine how arrays are used to store character strings.

LABORATORY 7: Cover Sheet

Date .... Section ....

Name ....

Place a checkmark in the *Assigned* column next to the exercises that your instructor has assigned to you. Have this sheet ready when your lab instructor checks your work. If your exercises are being checked outside the laboratory session, attach this sheet to the front of the packet of materials that you submit.

Exercise		*Assigned*	*Completed*
Prelab 1	Using Arrays		
Prelab 2	Passing Arrays to Functions		
Prelab 3	Strings		
Bridge	Testing and Debugging the Prelab Application Exercises *A Picture's Worth a Thousand Values* *Scaled Down* *Word of Fortune*		
In-lab 1	Applying Strings		
In-lab 2	Two-Dimensional Arrays		
Postlab	Searching Efficiently		
		Total	

Laboratory 7: Prelab Exercise 1

USING ARRAYS

Date .... Section ....

Name ....

BACKGROUND

An **array** is a named collection of data items. All the items in an array must be of the same type. You can create arrays of integers, arrays of characters, and so forth. An array declaration specifies the name of the array, the type of **elements** stored in the array, and the number of array elements (the size of the array). In the following program from the file *arrayio.cpp*, the array `polLevel` is used to store a set of pollution level readings.

```
// Reads six integers into array polLevel and displays them to
// the screen three per line.

#include <iostream.h>

void main()
{
    int polLevel[6];     // Array of six pollution level readings
    int j;               // Loop counter

    // Input six integers into the pollution level array.
    cout << "Enter the six pollution level readings: ";
    for ( j = 0; j < 6; j++ )
        cin >> polLevel[j];

    // Display the readings three values per line.
    for ( j = 0; j < 6; j++ )
    {
        if ( j % 3 == 0 )
            cout << endl;
        cout << polLevel[j] << " ";
    }
    cout << endl;
}
```

The declaration

```
int polLevel[6];
```

creates an array of integers named `polLevel` and reserves enough memory to store six integers.

The elements in an array are numbered beginning with zero. You refer to an individual array element by placing its number—called its **subscript** or **array index**—within square brackets immediately after the array name. You denote the first element in the `polLevel` array as `polLevel[0]`, the second as `polLevel[1]`, and so forth.

In the preceding program, a series of pollution level readings are input using a loop in which the loop counter, `j`, ranges from 0 to 5. For each value of `j`, the statement

```
cin >> polLevel[j];
```

reads in a pollution level and stores it in array element `polLevel[j]`. For example, if you entered the integer values

```
40 25 15 12 31 43
```

as the six pollution-level readings, your input data would be stored in `polLevel` as follows:

polLevel[0]	40
polLevel[1]	25
polLevel[2]	15
polLevel[3]	12
polLevel[4]	31
polLevel[5]	43

WARM-UP EXERCISE

Complete the following program by filling in the missing C++ code. A shell for this program is given in the file *scoreavg.shl*.

```
// Finds the average of up to 100 scores.

#include <iostream.h>
#include <iomanip.h>

const int MAX_NUM_SCORES = ____________        // Max number of scores

void main ()
{
    int count,                                // Actual number of scores
        j;                                    // Loop counter
    double score[________________],           // Array of size MAX_NUM_SCORES
           sumOfScores;                       // Sum of array elements

    // Prompt the user for the number of scores.
    cout << endl << "Enter the number of scores: ";
    cin >> count;

    // Read in the scores and store them in the array.
    cout << "Enter the scores: " << endl;
    for ( j = __; j < __________; j++ )
        cin >> ________;
    cout << endl;
```

```
    // Find and display the average of the scores.
    for (  j = __; j < __________; j++ )
        _______________________________;    // Sum the scores
    cout << "The average is " << setprecision(2)
         << sumOfScores / count << endl;
}
```

A PICTURE'S WORTH A THOUSAND VALUES

Data is often easier to interpret when it is displayed in a graphic form. Pie charts, line graphs, and bar charts are all examples of graphic representations of data. In this exercise you generate bar graphs like the one displayed below:

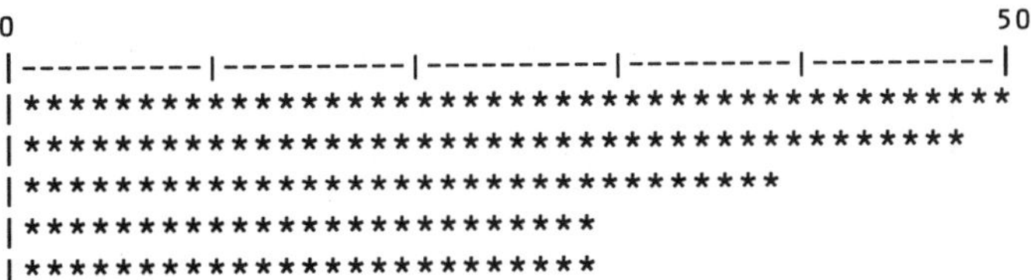

Step 1: Create a program that displays a bar graph from a set of integer values entered by the user. The user first enters the number of bars in the graph, followed by a set of integer values (one per bar). Your program then displays a bar graph in which each bar is formed using a row of asterisks. For example, a row representing the integer value 38 would contain 38 asterisks. Assume that the graph can have no more than 10 bars and that the integer values range from 0 to 50.

Input: The number of bars (up to 10)
A list of integer values in the range 0 to 50

Output: A bar graph

Be sure to display the bar graph scale (0–50) shown in the preceding bar graph.

Step 2: Save your program as *bar1.cpp*.

Step 3: Complete the following test plan.

Test Plan for *bar1*			
Test case	*Data*	*Expected result*	*Checked*

Bar graph with the max data value	5
	25
	50
	42
	40
	31
		`0                                                  50`
		`|-----|-----|-----|-----|-----|-----|-----|-----|-----|-----|`
		`|*************************`
		`|**************************************************`
		`|******************************************`
		`|****************************************`
		`|*******************************`	

Bar graph with the max number of bars			

Laboratory 7: Prelab Exercise 2

PASSING ARRAYS TO FUNCTIONS

Date .... Section ....

Name ....

BACKGROUND

When you call a function with an integer argument, a copy of the argument is created, and this copy is passed to the function. Passing arrays in this way is quite costly in terms of both the time it takes to create the copy and the memory required to store the copy. For the sake of efficiency, C++ uses a different mechanism, called **pass-by-reference**, to pass array arguments to functions.

When an array argument is passed to a function, the function is given the address in memory where the first element in the array is stored. As a result, changes made to the corresponding array parameter change the array argument also. The following program from the file *arrpass.cpp* passes an array argument to a function that modifies the contents of the array.

```
// Passes an array to a function and doubles the values in the array.

#include <iostream.h>

const int MAX_NUM_VALS = 20;   // Max number of data values
const int MAX_PER_LINE = 5;    // Max values per line to display

void inputValues ( int data[], int count );
void doubleValues ( int data[], int count );
void displayValues ( int data[], int count );

void main ()
{
    int numVals,                // Actual number of values to process
        value[MAX_NUM_VALS];    // Array of integers

    // Prompt the user for the number of data items.
    cout << endl << "Enter the number of values to process: ";
    cin >> numVals;

    // Read in the data.
    inputValues(value,numVals);

    // Double the value of each data element.
    doubleValues(value,numVals);
```

```
    // Display the data.
    cout << "Data doubled:";
    displayValues(value,numVals);
    cout << endl;
}

//----------------------------------------------------------------------

void inputValues ( int data[], int count )
// Read the values into an array.
{
    int j;
    cout << "Enter the data: ";
    for ( j = 0; j < count; j++ )
        cin >> data[j];
}

//----------------------------------------------------------------------

void doubleValues ( int data[], int count )
// Double values in the array.
{
    int j;
    for ( j = 0; j < count; j++ )
        data[j] = data[j] * 2;
}

//----------------------------------------------------------------------

void displayValues ( int data[], int count )
// Display the values in the array.
{
    int j;
    for ( j = 0; j < count; j++ )
    {
        if ( j % MAX_PER_LINE == 0 )
            cout << endl;
        cout << data[j] << " ";
    }
}
```

Let's look at the `inputValues()` function. The empty square brackets after `data` in the function prototype

```
inputValues ( int data[], int numVals );
```

signal the compiler that `data` is an array. The call

```
inputValues(value,numVals);
```

passes the array `value` to the parameter array `data`. In effect, `data` is nothing more than an alias for `value`. Any changes that are made to `data` in `inputValues()` are actually made to `value`. The same is true for the following call:

```
doubleValues(value,numVals);
```

This use of pass-by-reference is reflected in the following sample output:

```
Enter the number of values to process: 7
Enter the data: 34 50 43 21 39 46 44
Data doubled
68 100 86 42 78
92 88
```

WARM-UP EXERCISE

The following specifications describe functions that read in mileage data for a series of trips, convert the distance traveled from miles to kilometers for each trip, and display the length of each trip in both miles and kilometers.

`void readMileage ( double tripMiles[], int count )`

Input parameter
`count:` number of trips

Output parameter
`tripMiles[]:` number of miles in each trip (read from keyboard)

`void milesToKms ( double tripMiles[], double tripKms[], int count )`

Input parameters
`count:` number of trips
`tripMiles[]:` number of miles in each trip

Output parameter
`tripKms[]:` number of kilometers in each trip

`void displayData ( double tripMiles[], double tripKms[], int count )`

Input parameters
`count:` number of trips
`tripMiles[]:` number of miles in each trip
`tripKms[]:` number of kilometers in each trip

Outputs
Displays each trip in both miles and kilometers.

Complete the following program by filling in the missing C++ code. A shell for this program is given in the file *mile_km.shl*.

```
// Displays the distances travelled for up to 100 trips in both miles
// and kilometers.

#include <iostream.h>
#include <iomanip.h>
```

```
const int MAX_TRIPS = 100;           // Max number of trips
const double MILES_TO_KMS = 1.61;    // Miles to kilometers conversion
                                     // factor

// Function prototypes
void readMiles ( double tripMiles[], int count );
void milesToKms ( double tripMiles[], double tripKms[], int count );
void displayData ( double tripMiles[], double tripKms[], int count );

void main ()
{
    int numTrips;                   // Actual number of trips
    double miles[MAX_TRIPS],        // Miles data
           kms[MAX_TRIPS];          // Kilometers data

    // Prompt the user for the number of trips.
    cout << endl << "Enter the number of trips: ";
    cin >> numTrips;

    // Read the mileage for each trip.
    readMiles(_________________);

    // Convert from miles to kilometers.
    milesToKms(_________________________);

    // Display the data for each trip.
    displayData(_________________________);
}

//----------------------------------------------------------------------

void readMiles ( double tripMiles[], int count )
{
   int j;
   cout << "Enter the mileage for each trip: ";
   for ( j = 0; j < count; j++ )
       cin >> ______________;
}

//----------------------------------------------------------------------

void milesToKms ( double tripMiles[], double tripKms[], int count )
{
    int j;
    for ( j = 0; j < count; j++ )
    ______________ = ______________ * ______________;
}

//----------------------------------------------------------------------
```

```
void displayData ( double tripMiles[], double tripKms[], int count )
{
    int j;
    cout << endl << setw(4) << "Trip" << setw(7) << "Miles"
         << setw(12) << "Kilometers" << endl;
    for ( ___________________________________________ )
    {
       cout << setw(4) << j + 1
            << setw(7) << _____________________
            << setw(12) << _____________________
            << endl;
    }
}
```

SCALED DOWN

The bar graph program you created in Prelab Application Exercise 1 could only display integer values in the range 0 to 50. In this exercise you generalize your program to support a much broader range of values by scaling the data before displaying it. The data values are scaled to the range 0 to 50 using the following formula:

$$\textit{Scaled value} = \textit{data value} \cdot \frac{50}{\textit{maximum data value}}$$

Scaling the values 800, 1000, 600, and 700 using this formula produces the scaled values 40, 50, 30, and 35, respectively. Note that the maximum data value (1000) yields a scaled value of 50, and the remaining values are reduced linearly in proportion to the maximum data value.

Having scaled the data, your new program will then display it. The values listed above produce the following scaled bar graph:

```
0                                               1000
|---------|---------|---------|---------|---------|
|****************************************
|**************************************************
|******************************
|***********************************
```

Step 1: Using your program *bar1.cpp* as a basis, create a program that displays a scaled bar graph. Base your new program on the functions specified below:

`void readData ( double data[], int numValues )`

Input parameter

`numValues:` number of values (bars)

Output parameter

`data[]:` data values (read from keyboard)

`double maxDataValue ( double data[], int numValues )`

Input parameters

`data[]:` data values

`numValues:` number of values (bars)

Returns

The largest data value

```
void scaleValues ( double data[], int scaledData[],
                   int numValues, double maxValue   )
```

Input parameters

`data[]:` data values

`numValues:` number of values (bars)

`maxValue:` largest data value

Output parameter

`scaledData[]:` scaled data values

```
void displayBarGraph ( int scaledData[], int numValues,
                       double maxValue                    )
```

Input parameters
`scaledData[]:` scaled data values
`numValues:` number of values (bars)
`maxValue:` largest data value
Outputs
A scaled bar graph.

Step 2: Save your program as *bar2.cpp*.

Step 3: Complete the following test plan.

Test Plan for *bar2*			
Test case	*Data*	*Expected result*	*Checked*
Bar graph scaled by 50/100	 5 80 80.8 100 73 25	0 100 |-------------|-------------|-------------|-------------|-------------
** |** |** |************************************* |************	
Bar graph scaled by 50/2500			

Laboratory 7: Prelab Exercise 3

STRINGS

Date .... Section ....

Name ....

BACKGROUND

A **string** is a sequence of characters. You have been using one kind of string, string literals, to produce labeled output since Lab 1. A **string literal** is one or more characters enclosed in double quotes (e.g., `"A string"`). Although you didn't know it at the time, your string literals were represented using an array of characters. In this lab you learn how to manipulate character arrays.

You declare a character array in the same way you declare arrays that hold numeric data—you specify the type (`char`), name, and size of the array. The following array declaration

```
char firstName[10];
```

declares an array of 10 characters. You can store a string in this array as part of the array declaration:

```
char firstName[10] = "Bjarne";
```

or by reading in a string using `cin` and the >> operator:

```
char firstName[10];
...
cin >> firstName;
```

Note that you must enclose the string literal `"Bjarne"` within double quotes in order to distinguish it from the identifier `Bjarne`. When inputting the string `"Bjarne"` from the keyboard, however, you do *not* include the quotes.

The characters in the resulting string are stored starting in array element 0. The string `"Bjarne"` is stored in array `firstName` as follows:

firstName[0]	'B'
firstName[1]	'j'
firstName[2]	'a'
firstName[3]	'r'
firstName[4]	'n'
firstName[5]	'e'
firstName[6]	'/0'
firstName[7]	
firstName[8]	
firstName[9]	

A special character called the **null character** is used to mark the end of the string. The null character has the ASCII value zero and is represented as `'\0'`. This character is used to indicate that the remaining elements in the array are not part of the string. The null character is automatically included when a string is stored in a character array as part of an array declaration or when a string is read from the `cin` input stream. Note that a character array of size 10 can only store a string of 9 characters because room must be left for the null character.

When you display a string using `cout`, characters are displayed until the null character is encountered. The statement

```
cout << firstName << "++" << endl;
```

for example, produces the following output:

```
Bjarne++
```

Strings are commonly used to store words—commands, parameters, and so forth. As a result, the >> operator automatically treats **whitespace**—spaces, tabs, and the newline marker—in the input stream as **string delimiters**. Using the statement

```
cin >> firstName;
```

to read in

```
Bjarne Stroustrup
```

from the keyboard results in "`Bjarne`" being assigned to `firstName`. The space between the names terminates the input process for `firstName`. To read in both the first and last names, all you need to do is add another array to the `cin` statement:

```
cin >> firstName >> lastName;
```

In this case, the **newline marker**—the end of the input line—terminates the input process for `lastName`, resulting in `"Stroustrup"` being assigned to `lastName`.

The characters in a string can be manipulated in the same way as elements in any other array. You access individual characters using the array name and the appropriate subscript. The following code fragment outputs the third character in the `firstName` string and changes the first character of the string to `'b'`:

```
cout << firstName[2];
firstName[0] = 'b';
```

WARM-UP EXERCISE

Complete the following program by filling in the missing C++ code. A shell for this program is given in the file *backword.shl.*

```
// Displays the letters in a word in reverse order.

#include <iostream.h>

const int MAX_SIZE = ____;    // Max word size of five, allow for '\0'
void reverse ( char word[] );

void main()
{
        char word[_________];  // Array storing a word

        cout << endl << "Enter a word containing five letters or less: ";
        cin >> word;
        reverse(word);
}

void reverse ( char word[] )
{
     int i,
         lastCharPos = 0;    // Index of last letter in word

     // Find the end of the word.
     while ( word[lastCharPos] != _______ )
           lastCharPos++;

     // Display the word backwards.
     cout << "The word written backwards is: ";
     for ( i = ___________; i >= __; i-- )
           cout << _______;
     cout << endl
}
```

WORD OF FORTUNE

In this exercise you create a two-person version of the "Hangman" word-guessing game. The game begins with one player entering a secret word that is scrolled off the screen before the other player sits down to play. A blank guess template then appears on the screen. This template is the same length as the secret word but has dashes in place of the letters in the word.

The player attempting to guess the secret word enters letters one at a time. After each guess, the guess template is updated to show which letters in the secret word match the letter guessed (if any). For example, if the secret word is `"paper"`, guessing the letter `'p'` results in the following changes in the guess template:

```
Enter the secret word: paper  (This scrolls off the screen)

-----
Guess a letter: p
p-p--
```

This process continues until the guess template matches the secret word. The number of guesses is then output. A sample game is shown below.

```
Enter the secret word: test  (This scrolls off the screen)

----
Guess a letter: a
----
Guess a letter: e
-e--
Guess a letter: n
-e--
Guess a letter: s
-es-
Guess a letter: t
test=test
You guessed the word in 5 guesses
```

The program shell in the file *hangman.shl* contains the basic elements of the "Hangman" game. It is missing three key functions, however. Specifications for these functions are given below:

`void createTemplate ( char secretWord[], char guessTemplate[] )`

Input parameter

`secretWord[]:` the secret word

Output parameter

`guessTemplate[]:` a guess template containing all dashes

`void updateTemplate ( char secretWord[], char guessLetter, char guessTemplate[] )`

Input parameters

`secretWord[]:` the secret word

`guessLetter:` the letter guessed

Input/output parameter

`guessTemplate[]:` (input) a guess template showing the position of the letters guessed that match letters in the secret word
(output) an updated guess template that includes the letters in the secret word that match `guessletter`

`int matchTemplate ( char secretWord[], char guessTemplate[] )`

Input parameters

`secretWord:` the secret word

`guessTemplate[]:` a guess template showing the position of the letters guessed that match letters in the secret word

Returns

Returns 1 if the guess template is the same as the secret word. Otherwise, returns 0.

Step 1: Create the functions `createTemplate()`, `updateTemplate()`, and `matchTemplate()` specified above, and add them to the program shell in the file *hangman.shl.*

Step 2: Save your program in the file *hangman.cpp.*

Step 3: Complete the following test plan.

Test Plan for *hangman*			
Test case	*Sample data*	*Expected result*	*Checked*

test	`a e n s t`	`----`
		`----`
		`-e--`
		`-e--`
		`-es-`
		`test=test`
		You guessed the word in 5 guesses	

cryptic	`a e i o u y n s t r h c p`		
Your secret word			

Laboratory 7: Bridge Exercise

TESTING AND DEBUGGING THE PRELAB APPLICATION EXERCISES

Date .... Section ....

Name ....

Ask your instructor whether you need to complete this exercise before your lab session or during lab.

A PICTURE'S WORTH A THOUSAND VALUES

Step 1: Execute your program in the file *bar1.cpp*.

Step 2: Check each case in your *bar1* test plan, and verify the expected result. If you discover mistakes in your program, correct them and execute the test plan again.

SCALED DOWN

Step 1: Execute your program in the file *bar2.cpp*.

Step 2: Check each case in your *bar2* test plan, and verify the expected result. If you discover mistakes in your program, correct them and execute the test plan again.

WORD OF FORTUNE

Step 1: Execute your program in the file *hangman.cpp*.

Step 2: Check each case in your *hangman* test plan, and verify the expected result. If you discover mistakes in your program, correct them and execute the test plan again.

Laboratory 7: In-lab Exercise 1
APPLYING STRINGS

Date .... Section ....

Name ....

WHERE ARE YOU ON THE INFORMATION AUTOBAHN?

Many of you have received electronic mail (e-mail) from someone at a different location via the Internet. Have you ever been curious about the significance of the different fields in their e-mail addresses? One common form of Internet e-mail address is

user@system.domain.org

where *user* is the person's username, *system* is the name of his or her computer system, *domain* is the name of the organization with which the person is associated, and *org* is the type of organization. For example, the e-mail address of one of the authors of this lab book is

roberge@iitmax.iit.edu

where the username is *roberge*, the computer system is *iitmax*, the domain is *iit*, and the type of organization is *edu*. In some addresses, the domain section may include subdomains. For example, you can reach the other author at

cssmith@karl.acc.iit.edu

Step 1: Create a program that displays the fields following the @ symbol in an Internet e-mail address.

Input: The *system.domain.org* portion of an Internet address

Output: Displays each field of the address on a separate line

Step 2: Save your program as *internet.cpp.*

Step 3: Complete the following test plan.

Test Plan for *internet*			
Test case	*Sample data*	*Expected result*	*Checked*
Number of fields: four	`karl.acc.iit.edu`		
Number of fields: three	`iitmax.iit.edu`		
Number of fields: two	`aol.com`		
Your e-mail address			
E-mail address of a friend at a site (location) different from yours			

Laboratory 7: In-lab Exercise 2

Two-Dimensional Arrays

Date .... Section ....

Name ....

Your Name in Lights

There are many programming applications in which you naturally organize data into rows and columns. In C++ you can use a **two-dimensional array** to store data in this form. A declaration for a two-dimensional array of characters consisting of 5 rows and 11 columns is shown below:

```
char box[5][11]
```

The first array subscript specifies the number of rows, and the second specifies the number of columns. You identify a particular character using its row and column. For example, the assignment statement

```
box[2][3] = '*';
```

stores an asterisk in the element in the third row and fourth column of `box`—remember that indexing for both the row and the column starts at zero.

In this exercise you use a two-dimensional array of characters to represent a message board on which you place large block letters. For example, you can display the message `"I C U"` on a 5 × 11 message board as follows:

```
...........
.I.CCC.U.U.
.I.CC..U.U.
.I.CCC.UUU.
...........
```

The following function, `fillRectangle()`, fills in a specified rectangle on a message board with a given character.

```
void fillRectangle ( char board[NUM_ROWS][NUM_COLS],
                     int row, int col, int width,
                     int height, char fillChar      )
```

Input parameters

`row, col:` row and column of the upper, left-hand corner of the rectangle
`width, height:` rectangle dimensions
`fillChar:` character with which to fill the rectangle

Input/output parameter

`board[][]:` (input) message board
(output) updated message board including the specified rectangle

The `displayBoard()` function displays the message board:

`void displayBoard ( char board[NUM_ROWS][NUM_COLS] )`
Input parameter
`board[][]:` message board
Outputs
Displays the message board:

The following calls

```
fillRectangle(board,0,0,11,5,'.');    // Set the board to all '.'s
fillRectangle(board,1,1,1,3,'I');     // Forms the block letter 'I'
```

produce part of the message board shown above.

Step 1: Create the functions `fillRectangle()` and `displayBoard()` specified above.

Step 2: Add your functions to the test program *testbrd.cpp*.

Step 3: Test your functions using the following test plan. If you discover mistakes in your functions, correct them and execute the test plan again.

Test Plan for *displayBoard()* and *fillRectangle()*			
Test case	*Sample data*	*Expected result*	*Checked*
Data in test program	See the test program in file *testbrd.cpp*		

Laboratory 7: Postlab Exercise

SEARCHING EFFICIENTLY

Date .... Section ....

Name ....

PART A

What is the maximum number of IDs you would need to check in order to find a student ID in an *unsorted* array of 100 student IDs? Explain your reasoning behind your answer.

PART B

What is the maximum number of IDs you would need to check in order to find a student ID in a *sorted* array of 100 student IDs? Explain the reasoning behind your answer.

Structures and Searching

OVERVIEW

In Laboratory 7 you used arrays to represent collections of elements in which each element is of the same type. In this lab you use structures (`structs`) to represent collections in which the elements can be of different types. These structures provide you with a means of creating your own data types.

In Prelab Exercise 1, you examine how to define a structure, how to declare structure variables, and how to reference the individual elements in a structure variable. In Prelab Exercise 2, you learn how to pass structure variables to functions and how to create arrays in which each element is a structure. In Prelab Exercise 3, you create functions that search for a particular entry in an array of structures.

LABORATORY 8: Cover Sheet

Date .... Section ....

Name ....

Place a checkmark in the *Assigned* column next to the exercises that your instructor has assigned to you. Have this sheet ready when your lab instructor checks your work. If your exercises are being checked outside the laboratory session, attach this sheet to the front of the packet of materials that you submit.

Exercise		*Assigned*	*Completed*
Prelab 1	Simple Structures		
Prelab 2	Using Structures		
Prelab 3	Linear Search		
Bridge	Testing and Debugging the Prelab Application Exercises *Fit for Life* *Check the Label* *Have a Nice Day*		
In-lab 1	Returning a Structure from a Function		
In-lab 2	Binary Search		
Postlab	Comparing Arrays and Structures		
		Total	

Laboratory 8: Prelab Exercise 1

SIMPLE STRUCTURES

Date .... Section...

Name...

BACKGROUND

A **structure** is a collection of elements of various types. Each of the elements in a structure is called a **data member** and is referred to by name rather than by number, as was the case with arrays. Suppose that you wish to construct a data type consisting of a pair of integers that specify the *x*- and *y*-coordinates of a two-dimensional point. You can use a structure to create your own `Point` data type as follows:

```
// Definition of the Point data type
struct Point
{
   int x,   // Point coordinates
       y;
};
```

The definition of the `Point` structure begins with the keyword `struct`, followed by the structure name (`Point`). The declarations of the structure's data members (`x` and `y`) are enclosed within braces. Note that a semicolon follows the closing brace at the end of the structure definition. It is very easy to forget to include this semicolon, and omitting it will often cause the compiler to generate seemingly obscure error messages—especially when you break a program into multiple files (as you will do in Laboratory 9).

Once you have defined a data type using a structure, you declare a variable of this type just as you would declare a variable of any of C++'s built-in data types. For example, the declaration

```
Point pt1, pt2;
```

creates two variables (pt1 and pt2) of type Point. You access a variable's data members using the **dot operator** (.) followed by the name of a data member. The statement

```
pt1.x = 2;
```

assigns the value 2 to the x member of pt1. This value is used in the statement

```
pt1.y = pt1.x * pt1.x;
```

to specify the value of `pt1`'s *y*-coordinate. The following diagram shows `pt1`'s data members after execution of these statements:

```
      x  y
pt1 | 2  4 |
```

WARM-UP EXERCISE

Complete the following program by filling in the missing C++ code. A shell for this program is given in the file *sturec.shl*.

```
#include <iostream.h>

// Computes a student's grade point average (GPA).

// Definition of the Student data type
struct Student
{
   int IDNum,           // Student ID
       creditPts,       // Credit points
       creditHrs;       // Credit hours
   double GPA;          // Grade point average
};

void main()
{
   __________ _______;   // Declare a variable of type Student

   cout << endl << "Enter the student's ID, credit points,"
                << " and credit hours earned : ";
   cin >> ____________ >> ____________ >> ____________;

   // Calculate the student's GPA.

   ________________________________________________________;

   // Display the student data.

   cout << "Student ID:     " << ______________ << endl;
   cout << "Credit points:  " << ______________ << endl;
   cout << "Credit hours:   " << ______________ << endl;
   cout << "GPA:            " << ______________ << endl;
}
```

FIT FOR LIFE

You can compute a person's fitness level based on the time it takes the person to walk 3 miles *without* running. The following table gives the time standards for five general fitness levels for a woman 20 to 29 years old:

Fitness level (women, 20–29)	*Time it takes to walk 3 miles*
1	Over 48 minutes
2	Over 44 but less than or equal to 48 minutes
3	Over 40 but less than or equal to 44 minutes
4	Over 36 but less than or equal to 40 minutes
5	36 minutes or less

These standards can be extended to men by subtracting 2 minutes from each of the times listed above and to younger people aged 13 to 19 years by subtracting 1 minute from each time.

Step 1: Create a program that determines a person's fitness level based on the standards outlined above. Your program should read in the person's first name, last name, age, gender, and the length of time that it takes her or him to walk 3 miles. It should store the input information in a fitness profile structure, complete the contents of the structure by determining the person's fitness level, and output the completed fitness profile (first name, last name, age, gender, walk time, and fitness level). If the person's age falls outside the range 13 to 29 years old, your program should display a message indicating that the program cannot determine that person's fitness level.

Input: First name
Last name
Age (in years)
Gender (`'M'` or `'F'`)
Walk time (in minutes)

Output: Fitness profile (first name, last name, age, gender, walk time, and fitness level)

Step 2: Save your program as *fitness.cpp*.

Step 3: Complete the following test plan.

Test Plan for *fitness*			
Test case	*Sample data*	*Expected result*	*Checked*

Female, 22, 28-minute walk, fitness level 5	`Speedy Sara`
	`22`
	`F`
	`28`
		Name: Speedy Sara
		Age: 22 years old
		Gender: F
		Walk time: 28 minutes
		Fitness level: 5	

Male, 18, 40-minute walk, fitness level 3	`Andy Average`
	`18`
	`M`
	`40`
		Name: Andy Average
		Age: 18 years old
		Gender: M
		Walk time: 40 minutes
		Fitness level: 3	

Female, under 20, fitness level 2			
Male, over 20, fitness level 4			

Laboratory 8: Prelab Exercise 2

USING STRUCTURES

Date .... Section ....

Name ....

BACKGROUND

In this exercise you explore the use of structures as function parameters and array elements. You conclude by combining these concepts in the creation of functions that process an array of structures.

You declare a structure variable as a function parameter in exactly the same way you declare any other function parameter—you specify the type of parameter and the parameter name. For example, the prototype

```
double distance ( Point pt1, Point pt2 );
```

specifies a function that receives two parameters of type `Point`. Note that the default parameter passing mechanism for a structure is pass-by-value.

The `distance()` function uses `pt1`'s and `pt2`'s data members to compute the distance between these points as follows:

```
double distance ( Point pt1, Point pt2 )
// Returns the distance between two points.
{
    return  sqrt( pow((pt2.x-pt1.x),2) + pow((pt2.y-pt1.y),2) );
}
```

This function is used in the code fragment

```
Point alpha, beta;
...
cout << "Distance apart: " << distance(alpha,beta) << endl;
```

to compute the distance between two points `alpha` and `beta`.

In Laboratory 7 you created arrays of integers, characters, and so forth. You declare an array in which each element is a structure—an array of structures—by specifying a structure type followed by the name of the array and its size. The array declaration

```
Point pt[NUM_PTS];
```

creates an array named `pt` containing `NUM_PTS` points. Accessing the data members of an individual point in this array requires specifying the array index of the point followed by the name of a data member. The following loop assigns coordinate values to each point in the `pt` array:

```
for ( j = 0 ; j < NUM_PTS ; j++ )
    cin >> pt[j].x >> pt[j].y;
```

Suppose that NUM_PTS is 3. If the user enters the coordinate pairs

```
2 3
0 0
5 1
```

then the pt array contains the following data.

	x	y
pt[0]	2	3
pt[1]	0	0
pt[2]	5	1

The function displayDistances() takes an array of points as input and outputs the distance between each pair of points in the array. Note that the pt array is passed to displayDistances() using pass-by-reference.

```
void displayDistances ( Point pt[], int count )
// Displays the distance between each pair of points in the array.
// Parameter count is the number of points in the array. Note that
// each pair is only processed one time.
{
    for ( int j = 0 ; j < count-1 ; j++ )
        for ( int k = j+1 ; k < count ; k++ )
            cout << "Distance between points " << j << " and " << k
                 << " : " << distance(pt[j],pt[k]) << endl;
}
```

The distance() and displayDistances() functions are included in the program in the file *ptstruct.cpp*.

WARM-UP EXERCISE

Complete the following program by filling in the missing C++ code. A shell for this program is given in the file *stulist.shl*.

```
#include <iostream.h>
#include <iomanip.h>

// Displays information on a list of students.

const int MAX_STUDENTS = 100;    // Maximum number of students

// Definition of the Student data type
struct Student
{
   int IDNum,           // Student ID
       creditPts,       // Credit points
       creditHrs;       // Credit hours
   double GPA;          // Grade point average
};
```

```
// Function prototypes
void readStudentData ( Student stuList[], int count );
void calculateGPAs ( Student stuList[], int count );
void displayGPAs ( Student stuList[], int count );

void main()
{
   __________ __________[____________];   // Array of students
   int numStudents;                        // Number of students

   cout << endl << "Enter the number of students: ";
   cin >> numStudents;
   readStudentData(__________,___________);
   calculateGPAs(__________,___________);
   displayGPAs(_________,___________);
   cout << endl;
}

//--------------------------------------------------------------------

void readStudentData ( Student stuList[], int count )
// Reads in the ID numbers, credit points, and credit hours for a list
// of students and returns the information in the array stuList.
// Parameter count is the number of students.
{
   cout << endl << "Enter the ID number, credit points, and credit "
        << " hours for each student:" << endl;
   for ( ___________________________ )
       cin >> ______________________________________________;
}

//--------------------------------------------------------------------

void calculateGPAs ( Student stuList[], int count )
// Calculates the GPA for each student in the array. Parameter count
// is the number of students in the array.
{
   for ( ___________________________ )
       _____________________________________;
}

//--------------------------------------------------------------------

void displayGPAs ( Student stuList[], int count )
// Displays a table listing the ID number and GPA of each student in
// the array. Parameter count is the number of students in the array.
{
   cout << endl << setw(4) << "ID #" << setw(6) << "GPA" << endl;
   for ( ___________________________ )
       cout << setw(4) << _______________ << setprecision(2)
            << setw(6) << _______________ << endl;
}
```

CHECK THE LABEL

You used a bar graph in Laboratory 7 to graphically represent scaled data. In this exercise you add labels to the scaled bar graph that make the data more meaningful. A pair of labeled bar graphs representing the U.S. national debt and world population data for several major metropolitan areas are shown below.

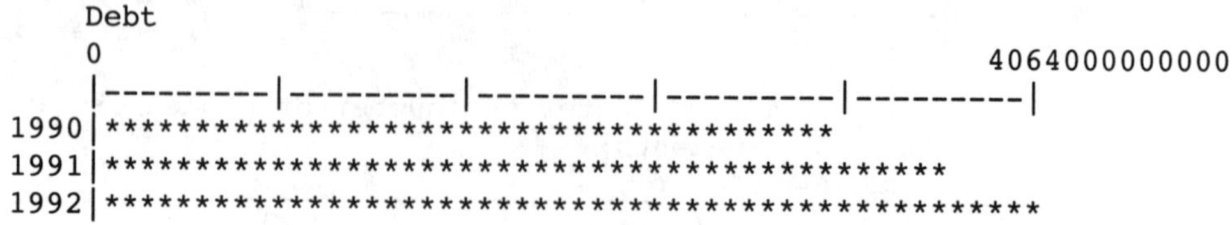

Step 1: Using your program *bar2.cpp* from Laboratory 7 as a basis, create a program that displays a labeled bar graph. Your program should begin by reading in a label for the graph—the label "Population" or "Debt" in the case of the graphs shown above. It also should read in a label for each bar as it reads in that bar's data. Assume that labels are at most 10 characters long.

Step 2: Save your program as *bar3.cpp*.

Step 3: Complete the following test plan.

Test Plan for *bar3*			
Test case	*Sample data*	*Expected result*	*Checked*

Populations of the world's largest metropolitan areas	`Population`
	`5`
	`Tokyo 28000000`
	`MexicoCity 23500000`
	`SaoPaolo 20900000`
	`Seoul 18600000`
	`NewYork 14630000`
		See the Population bar graph	

U.S. national debt	`Debt`
	`3`
	`1990 3233000000000`
	`1991 3665000000000`
	`1992 4064000000000`
		See the Debt bar graph	

Your own data			

Laboratory 8: Prelab Exercise 3

LINEAR SEARCH

Date .... Section ....

Name ....

BACKGROUND

Many applications require that you find a particular element in an array. The following function searches through the `list` array element by element until it finds an element that is equal to `searchKey`. If a matching element is found, then the function returns its array index. Otherwise, the function returns –1. This type of search is called a **linear search**. Note that the function stops the search as soon as `searchKey` is found.

```
int search ( int list[], int count, int searchKey )
// Linear search. Returns the array index of the entry that
// matches searchKey. Returns -1 if searchKey is not in the array.
// Parameter count is the number of elements in the array.
{
    int index = 0;  // Array index returned

    // Continue searching while there are more values left in the
    // array and searchKey has not been found.
    while ( index < count  &&  list[index] != searchKey )
           index++;

    // If index equals count, then the search failed.
    if ( index == count )
        index = -1;

    return index;
}
```

WARM-UP EXERCISE

Searches are commonly performed on arrays of structures. Usually, the search process focuses on a data member that identifies the entries in an array. The following program, for instance, uses a linear search to locate the student who has a specified student ID number. Complete this program by filling in the missing C++ code. A shell for this program is given in the file *stusrch.shl*.

```
#include <iostream.h>

// Retrieves student data.

const int MAX_STUDENTS = 100;   // Maximum number of students

// Definition of the Student data type
struct Student
{
   int IDNum,        // Student ID
       creditPts,    // Credit points
       creditHrs;    // Credit hours
   double GPA;       // Grade point average
};

// Function prototypes
void readStudentData ( Student stuList[], int count );  // From Ex. 2
void calculateGPAs ( Student stuList[], int count );  // From Ex. 2
int IDSearch ( Student stuList[], int count, int IDNumber );

void main()
{
   __________ __________[____________];   // Array of students
   int numStudents,                      // Number of students
       IDRequest,                        // Student ID to search for
       listIndex;                        // Array index of student
                                         //   with matching ID

   cout << endl << "Enter the number of students: ";
   cin >> numStudents;
   readStudentData(__________,___________);
   calculateGPAs(__________,___________);

   // Prompt the user for a student ID number.
   cout << endl << "Enter a student ID number: ";
   cin >> IDRequest;

   // If a student with this ID number is in the list, output
   // her or his GPA.
   listIndex = IDSearch(____________,____________,____________);
   if ( listIndex != -1 )
      cout << "The student's GPA is "
           << ___________________________________ << endl;
   else
      cout << "The student is not in the list." << endl;
}

//----------------------------------------------------------------------

int IDSearch ( Student stuList[], int count, int IDNumber )
// Linear search. Returns the array index of the entry for the
// student whose ID number matches IDNumber. Returns -1 if there is
// no such student. Parameter count is the number of students in the
// array.
{
```

```
    int index = 0;  // Array index returned

    // Continue searching while there are more students left in the
    // list and an ID matching IDNumber has not been found.
    while ( ______________________________________________ )
        _____________;

    // If index equals count, then the search failed.
    if ( index == count )
        index = -1;

    return index;
}
```

If you know that the data in an array is sorted in ascending order, then you can improve the efficiency of the linear search algorithm somewhat by stopping the search whenever you encounter a value that is larger than the value you are searching for. After all, there is no point in searching the remainder of the array, all these values must be greater than the value you are searching for.

Add this modification to the `IDSearch()` function you completed above. Assume that the array of students is sorted in ascending order based on student ID. Note that you need to change both the while condition that controls the search and the if condition that determines whether the search terminated unsuccessfully.

```
int IDSearch ( Student stuList[], int count, int IDNumber )
// Linear search of an array of students that is sorted in ascending
// order based on student ID number. Returns the array index of the
// entry for the student whose ID number matches IDNumber.
// Returns -1 if there is no such student. Parameter count is the
// number of students in the array.
{
    int index = 0;  // Array index returned

    // Continue searching while there are more students left in the
    // list and an ID that is greater than or equal to IDNumber has
    // not been found.
    while ( ______________________________________________ )
        _____________;

    // Check if the search failed.
    if ( ________________________________ )
        index = -1;

    return index;
}
```

HAVE A NICE DAY

In this exercise you create a function that searches a list of holidays for a specified date and returns the name of the holiday (if any) associated with that date.

```
void findHoliday ( DayData holidayList[], int listLength,
                   int month, int day, char holiday[]    )
```

Input parameters
holidayList[]: list of holidays
listLength: number of entries in the list
month, day: month and day to search for
Output parameter
holiday: string containing the name of the holiday associated with the specified month/day or the empty string if there is no holiday associated with that date.

Each entry in the `holiday` array is a `DayData` structure containing a month (`month`), day (`day`), and holiday name (`holiday`).

```
struct DayData
{
   int month,
       day;
   char holiday[MAX_NAME_LEN];
}
```

A sample list of holidays from the file *holidays.dat* is shown below:

holidayList[0]	1 11 Hostos Day (Puerto Rico)
holidayList[1]	1 15 Martin Luther King Jr. Day
holidayList[2]	1 23 Handwriting Day
holidayList[3]	2 3 Setsubun bean-throwing festival (Japan)
holidayList[4]	2 5 Cham Cham Mapinduzi Day (Tanzania)
holidayList[5]	2 6 Babe Ruth's Birthday
holidayList[6]	2 9 Feast of Saint Appolonia (patron saint of dentists)
holidayList[7]	2 10 Feast of St. Paul's Shipwreck (Malta)

Step 1: Create the function `findHoliday()` specified above. Assume that the list of holidays is sorted in ascending order according to date. Further assume that no date appears more than once in the list and that some dates are missing from the list. Note that the empty string consists of the null character (`'\0'`) alone.

Step 2: Add your `findHoliday()` function to the program shell in the file *holidays.shl*. This shell includes all the code needed to read in a list of holidays from the file *holidays.dat*. Save your program as *holidays.cpp*.

Step 3: Complete the following test plan.

Test Plan for *findHoliday()*			
Test case	*Sample data*	*Expected result*	*Checked*
Date appears in the list	`3 31`	Bunsen Burner Day	
Date does not appear in the list	`2 4`	No holiday listed	

Laboratory 8: Bridge Exercise

TESTING AND DEBUGGING THE PRELAB APPLICATION EXERCISES

Date .... Section ....

Name ....

Ask your instructor whether you need to complete this exercise before your lab session or during lab.

FIT FOR LIFE

Step 1: Execute your program in the file *fitness.cpp*.

Step 2: Check each case in your *fitness* test plan, and verify the expected result. If you discover mistakes in your program, correct them and execute the test plan again.

CHECK THE LABEL

Step 1: Execute your program in the file *bar3.cpp*.

Step 2: Check each case in your *bar3* test plan, and verify the expected result. If you discover mistakes in your program, correct them and execute the test plan again.

HAVE A NICE DAY

Step 1: Execute your program in the file *holidays.cpp*.

Step 2: Check each case in your *findHoliday()* test plan, and verify the expected result. If you discover mistakes in your function, correct them and execute the test plan again.

Laboratory 8: In-lab Exercise 1

RETURNING A STRUCTURE FROM A FUNCTION

Date .... Section ....

Name ....

ONE RINGY-DINGY, TWO RINGY-DINGY

Each key on a telephone keypad generates a different pair of tones. One tone is determined by the row on which the key appears, and the other is determined by the column. The frequencies of these tones are listed below:

	Key			*Row tone (Hz)*
	1	2	3	697
	4	5	6	770
	7	8	9	852
	*	0	#	941
Column tone (Hz)	1209	1336	1477	

For example, pressing the 8 key generates a row tone at 852 Hz and a column tone at 1336 Hz.

Step 1: Create a function `keyTones()` that returns a structure containing the row tone and column tone produced by a given key. Base your function on the following specification:

`PhoneTones keyTones ( char key )`
Input parameter
`key:` the key pressed (`'0'`-`'9'`, `'*'`, or `'#'`)
Returns
The tones produced by that key.

The `PhoneTones` structure is defined below:

```
struct PhoneTones
{
   int rowTone,    // Frequencies of the tones generated by a key press
       colTone;
};
```

Step 2: Add your `keyTones()` function to the test program *testtone.cpp*.

Step 3: Test your `keyTones()` function using the following test plan. If you discover mistakes in your function, correct them and execute the test plan again.

Test Plan for *keyTones()*

Test case	*Sample data*	*Expected result*	*Checked*
Row 1, Column 3	3	Tones produced at 697 and 1477 Hz	
Row 2, Column 2	5	Tones produced at 770 and 1336 Hz	

Laboratory 8: In-lab Exercise 2

BINARY SEARCH

Date .... Section ....

Name ....

SPLITTING THE DIFFERENCE

In Prelab Exercise 3 you used a linear search to locate a value in an array. If the array is sorted, however, you can use a much more efficient search, called a **binary search**, to locate values. Unlike the linear search algorithm, the binary search algorithm does not simply iterate through the array entries from beginning to end. Instead, it rapidly narrows the range of array entries in which the value might lie until either it locates the value or it recognizes that there are no entries that might contain the value.

Suppose that you are given the following sorted array of integers

Array index	0	1	2	3	4	5	6	7	8	9	10	11	12	13	14	15
Array entry	4	7	11	15	23	29	35	37	42	46	51	54	67	72	78	86

and are asked to locate the value 46. At this point, the value 46 could lie anywhere within the array, so the initial search range is all 16 entries. We mark the beginning of this range using the variable `low` and the end using the variable `high`:

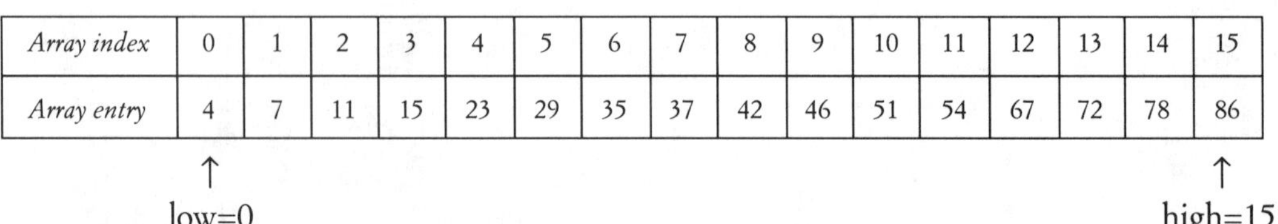

Array index	0	1	2	3	4	5	6	7	8	9	10	11	12	13	14	15
Array entry	4	7	11	15	23	29	35	37	42	46	51	54	67	72	78	86

How do you narrow the search range? You begin by locating the entry in the middle of the search range. The index of this entry is the average of indices `low` and `high`:

```
middle = ( low + high ) / 2;
```

If `low` is 0 and `high` is 15, then `middle` equals (0 + 15)/2, or 7:

Array index	0	1	2	3	4	5	6	7	8	9	10	11	12	13	14	15
Array entry	4	7	11	15	23	29	35	37	42	46	51	54	67	72	78	86

↑ low=0 ↑ middle=7 ↑ high=15

The array entry with index 7 is 37. You narrow the search range by comparing the value you are searching for—in this example, 46—with 37. The fact that 46 is greater than 37 indicates that you do not need to search through array entries 0 to 7 because these entries are less than or equal to 37 (the array is sorted) and are therefore less than 46. You reflect this narrowing of the search range by changing `low` as follows:

```
low = middle + 1;
```

yielding the result shown below. Note that you have halved the size of the search range with just one comparison.

Array index	0	1	2	3	4	5	6	7	8	9	10	11	12	13	14	15
Array entry	4	7	11	15	23	29	35	37	42	46	51	54	67	72	78	86

↑ low=8 ↑ high=15

You continue the search by repeating the process outlined above. The average of `low` and `high` is (8 + 15)/2, or 11:

Array index	0	1	2	3	4	5	6	7	8	9	10	11	12	13	14	15
Array entry	4	7	11	15	23	29	35	37	42	46	51	54	67	72	78	86

↑ low=8 ↑ middle=11 ↑ high=15

The array entry with index 11 is 54. The fact that 46 is less than 54 indicates that you do not need to search entries 11 to 15, for these entries are greater than or equal to 54 and thus are greater than 46. You therefore change `high` as follows:

```
high = middle - 1;
```

yielding the result shown below. Note that you have once again halved the search range.

Array index	0	1	2	3	4	5	6	7	8	9	10	11	12	13	14	15
Array entry	4	7	11	15	23	29	35	37	42	46	51	54	67	72	78	86

↑ low=8 ↑ high=15

In this case, the average of `low` and `high` is (8 + 10)/2, or 9:

Array index	0	1	2	3	4	5	6	7	8	9	10	11	12	13	14	15
Array entry	4	7	11	15	23	29	35	37	42	46	51	54	67	72	78	86
									↑ low	↑ middle	↑ high					

The array entry with index 9 is 46—the value you are searching for—so your search ends with success. More important, it only took three comparisons to locate 46.

In this exercise you further explore the functioning of the binary search algorithm using the following implementation from the file *binsrch.cpp*.

```
int binarySearch ( int list[], int count, int searchKey )

// Binary search of an array that is sorted in ascending order.
// Returns the array index of the entry that matches searchKey.
// Returns -1 if searchKey is not in the array. Parameter count is
// the number of elements in the array.

{
    int low   = 0,                // Low index of current search range
        high  = count - 1,        // High index of current search range
        middle,                   // Middle of the current search range
        found = 0;                // Flag indicating searchKey was found

    while ( low <= high  &&  !found )
    {
        middle = ( low + high ) / 2;               // Compute midpoint
        if ( searchKey < list[middle] )
           high = middle - 1;                      // Search lower half
        else if ( searchKey > list[middle] )
           low = middle + 1;                       // Search upper half
        else
           found = 1;                              // searchKey found
    }

    if ( !found )
       middle = -1;    // searchKey not found, adjust index returned

    return middle;
}
```

Step 1: The program in *binsrch.cpp* begins by generating an array containing the odd integers from 1 to 99. Use this program to complete the following table by filling in the intermediate values of variables `low`, `middle`, and `high`, as well as the result of each search.

Note that you must either use a debugger to trace through the program noting changes in the values of variables `low`, `middle`, and `high` as the program executes, or else you must add code that outputs the intermediate values of these variables.

Tracing the Execution of the *binarySearch()* Function			
Test case	*Search value*	*Intermediate results*	*Result returned*
Quick search	**75**	low 0 25 middle 24 37 high 49 49	37
Search goes longer	**41**	low middle high	
Search goes full depth	**53**	low middle high	
Search goes full depth	**9**	low middle high	
Search fails	**62**	low middle high	
Search fails	**22**	low middle high	

Step 2: For an array of a given length, there is an upper limit to the number of comparisons the `binarySearch()` function will make when searching for a value. Complete the following table by determining this limit for arrays containing 8, 16, 32, 64, and 128 entries. Note that you can change the length of the array in the program *binsrch.cpp* by changing the value of the constant `ARRAY_LENGTH`.

Array length	*Maximum number of comparisons required to locate a value*
8	3
16	
32	
64	
128	

Laboratory 8: Postlab Exercise

COMPARING ARRAYS AND STRUCTURES

Date .... Section ....

Name ....

In the past two laboratories you examined two methods for forming collections of data—arrays and structures—that exist in one form or another in most modern programming languages. The following table compares and contrasts the properties and uses of arrays and structures in C++.

	Arrays	*Structures*
Must all the data items in an array/structure be of the same type?		
How do you declare an array/structure variable? Give an example of each.		
How do you access a data item in an array/structure? Give an example of each.		
What form of parameter passing—pass-by-value or pass-by-reference—is used by default with arrays/structures?		

Classes I

OVERVIEW

In the last lab you used a structure to represent an aggregate data type containing a set of data members. In this lab you expand the concept of an aggregate data type by bundling data members and the functions that manipulate them into a single entity using the C++ class construct. Classes provide the foundation for object-oriented programming and distinguish C++ from traditional structured programming languages such as C, Pascal, and FORTRAN.

In Prelab Exercise 1, you learn how to declare and define a class, how to create class variables (objects), and how to implement member functions that access the information stored in an object's data members. In Prelab Exercise 2, you implement member functions that modify an object. Prelab Exercise 3 asks you to create functions that display two types of objects on the screen—points and text windows.

LABORATORY 9: Cover Sheet

Date .... Section ....

Name ....

Place a checkmark in the *Assigned* column next to the exercises that your instructor has assigned to you. Have this sheet ready when your lab instructor checks your work. If your exercises are being checked outside the laboratory session, attach this sheet to the front of the packet of materials that you submit.

Exercise		*Assigned*	*Completed*
Prelab 1	What Is a Class?		
Prelab 2	Modifying an Object		
Prelab 3	Displaying an Object		
Bridge	Testing and Debugging the Prelab Application Exercises *We Do Windows* *A Change for the Better* *Window Frame*		
In-lab 1	Using Multiple Objects		
In-lab 2	Applying the `TextWindow` Class		
Postlab	Designing Classes		
		Total	

Laboratory 9: Prelab Exercise

WHAT IS A CLASS?

Date .... Section ....

Name ....

BACKGROUND

The `Point` data type shown below consists of a pair of integers that specify the *x*- and *y*-coordinates of a two-dimensional point.

```
class Point
{
  ...
    int x,      // x-coordinate
        y;      // y-coordinate
};
```

In order to use variables of type `Point`, you need functions that perform basic actions such as initializing a point's coordinates, moving a point, displaying a point, and so forth. You could create functions called `movePoint()`, `displayPoint()`, etc. A more effective approach is to incorporate these functions as part of the `Point` data type. The result is a **class** consisting of a set of **data members** and a set of functions—called **member functions**—that manipulate these data members. The following class declaration from the file *point.h* includes several member functions that operate on two-dimensional points.

```
//  Declaration for a two-dimensional Point class.

class Point
{
  public:           // Member functions

    // Constructor
    Point ( int xCoord, int yCoord );       // Define a point

    // Derived point attribute
    double distance ();                     // Distance from (0,0)

    // Modification functions
    void move ( int dx, int dy );           // Move point
    void exchangeXY ();                     // Exchange coordinates

    // Point display function
    void display ();

    // Outputs the data members -- used in testing and debugging
    void showDataMembers ();
```

```
   private:        // Data members

     int x,        // x-coordinate
         y;        // y-coordinate
};
```

You declare a variable—or **object**—of type `Point` as follows:

```
Point pt(2,5);
```

This declaration creates an object with an *x*-coordinate of 2 and a *y*-coordinate of 5. In Laboratory 8 you used the dot operator (.) to access a structure's data members. In the case of classes, you use the dot operator both to access an object's data members and to call its member functions. For example, to display point `pt`, you use the name of the object followed by the dot operator and the member function to be invoked:

```
pt.display();
```

Several points (no pun intended) need to be made about the `Point` class declaration. The declaration includes a **public** section containing the prototypes for the class's member functions and a **private** section containing its data members. By making the data members private, you prevent functions that are not members of the `Point` class from directly accessing and manipulating a `Point` object's data members. The code fragment

```
void main ()
{
    Point pt(1,2);
    pt.x = 5;          // Error -- attempts to access private data member
}
```

produces a compilation error because `x` is a private data member and therefore can only be accessed by one of `Point`'s member functions. Indirect access to the data members is provided by `Point`'s member functions. These functions are public and thus can be called by any function—either member or nonmember. Collectively, the member functions provide a **public interface** to the `Point` class.

The `Point` class declaration lists the class's data members and member functions. In order to use the `Point` class, you must first implement its member functions. Let's start by looking at how we specify member functions. For each function, we give the preconditions (or **requirements**) that must exist before the function is called and the **results** of the function—that is, what value the function returns or what action the function performs. This style is used in the following function specifications.

`Point ( int xCoord, int yCoord )`

Requirements
None
Results
Constructor. Creates a point with coordinates `xCoord` and `yCoord`.

`double distance ()`

Requirements
None
Results
Returns the distance from a point to the origin (0, 0).

The first of these functions is a special member function called a **constructor**. A constructor allocates memory for an object and initializes its data members. The constructor for a given class is automatically called whenever an object of that class is declared in a program. The declaration

```
Point nextPt(2,4);
```

for example, invokes the `Point` class constructor, which initializes `nextPt`'s data members `x` and `y` to 2 and 4, respectively. Note that a constructor has the same name as the class to which it belongs—`Point`, in this case—and does not have a return type. An implementation of the `Point` class constructor is given below. The **scope resolution operator** (::) is used to signal the compiler that this function is a member function of the `Point` class.

```
Point::Point ( int xCoord, int yCoord )
{
    x = xCoord;
    y = yCoord;
}
```

The second function in the `Point` class, `distance()`, returns the distance from a point to the origin (0, 0).

```
double Point::distance ()
// Returns the distance from a point to the origin (0,0).
{
    return ( sqrt( pow(x,2) + pow(y,2) ) );
}
```

Once again, the scope resolution operator is used to indicate that this function is part of the `Point` class. Because `distance()` is a `Point` member function, it can reference the data members `x` and `y` directly. Note that you do not need to include `x` and `y` as parameters to the `distance ()` function.

The following code fragment contains a pair of calls to the `distance()` function.

```
void main ()
{
    Point alpha(1,2),
          beta(3,5);
    cout << alpha.distance() << endl;
    cout << beta.distance() << endl;
}
```

When the call `alpha.distance()` is made, the `distance()` function automatically uses `alpha`'s `x` and `y` data members—that is, `x` = 1 and `y` = 2—whereas for the call `beta.distance()`, it uses `beta`'s data members.

The declaration for a class and the implementation of its member functions are usually stored in separate files. The class declaration is stored in an appropriately named **header file**—*point.h* in the case of the `Point` class—and the implementation is stored in a similarly named source file. A copy of the file *point.cpp* containing an implementation of some of `Point`'s member functions is given below. The class declaration in *point.h* and the member function implementations in *point.cpp* combine to form the `Point` class

```
#include <iostream.h>
#include <math.h>
#include "point.h"

//--------------------------------------------------------------------

Point::Point ( int xCoord, int yCoord )
// Constructor.
{
    x = xCoord;
    y = yCoord;
}

//--------------------------------------------------------------------

double Point::distance ()
// Returns the distance from a point to the origin (0,0).
{
    return ( sqrt( pow(x,2) + pow(y,2) ) );
}

//--------------------------------------------------------------------

void Point::showDataMembers ()
// Displays a point's data members. Use for testing/debugging only.
{
    cout << "(" << x << " " << y << ")";
}
```

Note that any file that contains references to the `Point` class must include the header file *point.h* so that the compiler can resolve these references.

WARM-UP EXERCISE

The following `main()` function from the file *testpt.cpp* uses the `Point` class to compute the distance from a pair of points to the origin.

```
#include <iostream.h>
#include "point.h"

void main()
{
    // Construct the points (10,5) and (7,8).
    Point pt1(10,5),
          pt2(7,8);

    // Display both points' data members.
    cout << "Point 1: "; pt1.showDataMembers(); cout << endl;
    cout << "Point 2: "; pt2.showDataMembers(); cout << endl;

    // Display the distance from each point to (0,0).
    cout << "Distance from Point 1 to the origin: "
         << pt1.distance() << endl;
    cout << "Distance from Point 2 to the origin: "
         << pt2.distance() << endl;
}
```

The resulting program is formed from the contents of three files *testpt.cpp* (the `main()` function), *point.h* (the `Point` class declaration), and *point.cpp* (the implementations of `Point`'s member functions).

Step 1: Check your compiler's documentation to determine how to construct a multifile program.

Step 2: Compile the implementation of the `Point` class in the file *point.cpp*.

Step 3: Compile the test program in the file *testpt.cpp*.

Step 4: Link the object files produced by steps 2 and 3.

Step 5: Run the executable file produced by step 4.

WE DO WINDOWS

A **window** is a specially delineated area of the screen. In this lab's Prelab Application Exercises you implement a class that you can use to create, resize, move, and display windows containing text strings. The declaration for the `TextWindow` class from the file *twindow.h* is given below.

```
// TextWindow class declaration from twindow.h

const int MAX_TEXT_LENGTH = 101;    // Maximum length of a text string

class TextWindow
{
  public:

    // Constructor
    TextWindow ( int leftEdge, int topEdge,
                 int rightEdge, int bottomEdge,
                 char textString[]              );

    // Derived window attributes
    int width ();                              // Window width
    int height ();                             // Window height

    // Window modification functions
    void move ( int dx, int dy );              // Move a window
    void resize ( int dx, int dy );            // Resize a window
    void replaceText ( char textString[] );    // Replace window text

    // Outputs the data members -- used in testing and debugging
    void showDataMembers ();

    // Window display function
    void display ();
```

```
  private:

    // Data members
    int left,                        // Positions of the window's edges
        top,
        right,
        bottom;
    char text[MAX_TEXT_LENGTH];      // Window's text string
};
```

Step 1: Implement the following set of member functions:

`TextWindow ( int leftEdge, int topEdge, int rightEdge, int bottomEdge, char textString[] )`

Requirements
None
Results
Constructor. Creates a window that is bounded by the specified edges and contains `textString`.

`int width ()`

Requirements
None
Results
Returns the width of a window.

`int height ()`

Requirements
None
Results
Returns the height of a window.

Step 2: Save your implementations of these functions as the file *twindow.cpp*.

Step 3: Add the implementation of the member function `showDataMembers()` given in the file *showdata.cpp* to the file *twindow.cpp*.

Step 4: Complete the following test plan for the constructor, `width()`, and `height()` functions.

Test Plan for *Test 1*			
Test case	*Sample data*	*Expected result*	*Checked*
Construct a 40 x 10 (40 wide by 10 high) text window containing the text string "Sample"		top = left = right = bottom = text = Sample width = 40 height = 10	
Construct a 20 x 5 text window containing the text string "My text"		top = left = right = bottom = text = My text width = 20 height = 5	

Laboratory 9: Prelab Exercise 2

MODIFYING AN OBJECT

Date .... Section ....

Name ....

BACKGROUND

Although the user of an object does not have direct access to the object's private data members, you can create public member functions that provide indirect access so that the user can retrieve or modify private data members. The following member function moves a point by specified amounts in the *x*- and *y*-directions, thereby modifying the point's private data members `x` and `y`.

```
void Point::move ( int dx, int dy )
// Moves a point by the specified amounts.
{
    x += dx;
    y += dy;
}
```

The code fragment below, for example, moves point `pt`'s coordinates from (12, 4) to (8, 7).

```
// Construct a point with an initial x-coordinate of 12 and an
// initial y-coordinate of 4.
Point pt(12,4);

// Move pt's x-coordinate by -4 and pt's y-coordinate by +3.
pt.move(-4,3);
```

Note that `pt`'s data members are modified without making direct reference to them.

WARM-UP EXERCISE

The following member function exchanges a point's *x*- and *y*-coordinates.

`void exchangeXY ()`

Requirements
None
Results
Exchanges a point's *x*- and *y*-coordinates.

Complete the following function by filling in the missing C++ code. A shell for this function is given in the file *point.cpp*.

```
void ________::exchangeXY ()
{


}
```

A CHANGE FOR THE BETTER

In this exercise you add several member functions to your `TextWindow` class. Each of these member functions modifies a text window's private data members in a different way.

`void move ( int dx, int dy )`

Requirements
None
Results
Moves a window by the specified amounts.

`void resize ( int dx, int dy )`

Requirements
None
Results
Resizes a window by moving its lower, right-hand corner by the specified amounts.

`void replaceText ( char textString[] )`

Requirements
None
Results
Replaces a window's text with `textString`.

Step 1: Implement the `TextWindow` class member functions specified above. Prototypes for these functions are included in the declaration of the `TextWindow` class in the file *twindow.h*.

Step 2: Add these functions to your `TextWindow` class implementation in the file *twindow.cpp*.

Step 3: Complete the following test plan for the `move()` function.

Test Plan for *Test 2*			
Test case	*Sample data*	*Expected result*	*Checked*
Construct a 40 x 10 text window containing the text string "Sample"		top = left = right = bottom = text = Sample width = 40 height = 10	
Move the window constructed above 10 units horizontally and 2 units vertically	`10 2`	top = left = right = bottom = text = Sample width = 40 height = 10	
Move the window constructed above –5 units horizontally and –2 units vertically	`-5 -2`	top = left = right = bottom = text = Sample width = 40 height = 10	

Step 4: Complete the following test plan for the `resize()` function.

Test Plan for *Test 3*			
Test case	*Sample data*	*Expected result*	*Checked*
Construct a 40 x 10 text window containing the text string "Sample"		top = left = right = bottom = text = Sample width = 40 height = 10	
Make the window larger by 10 units horizontally and 2 units vertically	`10 2`	top = left = right = bottom = text = Sample width = 50 height = 12	
Make the window smaller by 5 units horizontally and 3 units vertically	`-5 -3`	top = left = right = bottom = text = Sample width = 35 height = 7	

Step 5: Complete the following test plan for the `replaceText()` function.

Test Plan for *Test 4*			
Test case	*Sample data*	*Expected result*	*Checked*
Construct a 40 x 10 text window containing the text string "Sample"		top = left = right = bottom = text = Sample width = 40 height = 10	
Replace the text string with "New Word"	`New word`	top = left = right = bottom = text = Sample width = 40 height = 10	
Replace the text string with your name		top = left = right = bottom = text = Sample width = 40 height = 10	

Laboratory 9: Prelab Exercise 3

DISPLAYING AN OBJECT

Date .... Section ....

Name ....

BACKGROUND

In this exercise you develop functions that display points and text windows on your computer screen. Most programming environments include functions that allow you to move the cursor to a specified position on the screen and to output text starting at that position. Before beginning this exercise, you need to determine what C++ functions your system provides for performing these tasks and how your screen coordinate system is organized—for example, what are the coordinates of the four corners of the screen?

WARM-UP EXERCISE

The following `Point` class member function displays an asterisk at the coordinates of a given point.

`void display ()`

Requirements
None
Results
Displays an asterisk on the screen at a point's coordinates.

Complete the following function by filling in the missing C++ code. A shell for this function is given in the file *point.cpp*.

```
void _______::display ()
// Displays a point as an asterisk (*) on the screen.
{







}
```

WINDOW FRAME

The following `TextWindow` member function displays a text window on the screen.

`void display ()`

Requirements
The window's edges lie within the screen boundaries.
Results
Displays a text window. Begins by displaying the window's border and then displays the window's text string within the border. Treats vertical bars (|) in the window's text string as end-of-line markers and crops the text to fit the window's borders.

A screen containing three text windows is shown below. Each window is labeled with its text string. Note the results produced by vertical bars in the bottom two windows and the cropping of the string by the small window on the right.

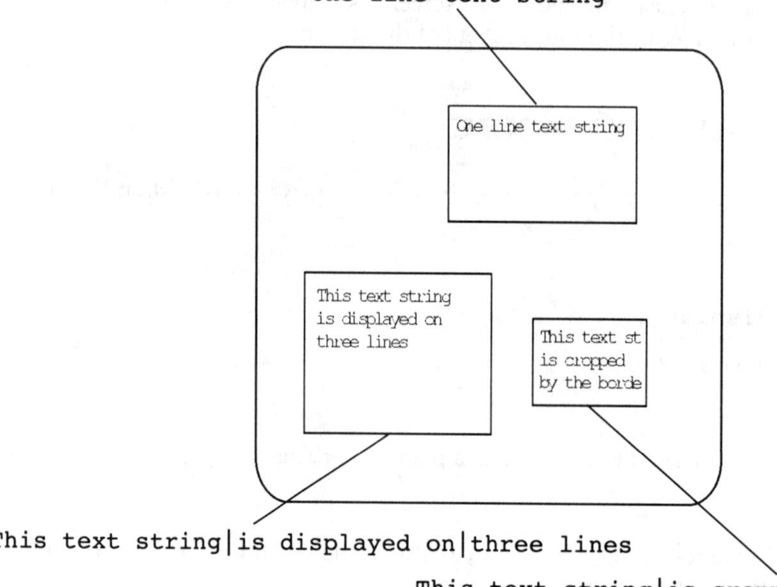

Step 1: Implement the `display()` member function specified above. A prototype for this function is included in the declaration of the `TextWindow` class in the file *twindow.h*.

Step 2: Add this function to your `TextWindow` class implementation in the file *twindow.cpp*.

Step 3: Complete the following test plan for the `display()` function.

Test Plan for *Test 5*			
Test case	*Sample data*	*Expected result*	*Checked*
Construct a 40 x 10 text window containing the text string "Sample"			
Display a text window containing a multiline text string			
Display a text window containing a cropped text string			

Laboratory 9: Bridge Exercise

TESTING AND DEBUGGING THE PRELAB APPLICATION EXERCISES

Date .... Section ....

Name ....

Check with your instructor whether you need to complete this exercise before your lab session or during lab.

Test your implementation of the `TextWindow` class using the test programs in the files *testwin1.cpp–testwin5.cpp.* These programs support the following tests.

Test	*Action*
1	Tests the constructor, `width()`, and `height()` functions
2	Tests the `move()` function
3	Tests the `resize()` function
4	Tests the `replaceText()` function
5	Tests the `display()` function

WE DO WINDOWS

Step 1: Compile your implementation of the `TextWindow` class (in the file *twindow.cpp*) and the test program in the file *testwin1.cpp.* Link the resulting object files to produce an executable file.

Step 2: Check each case in the test plan for *Test 1* (constructor, `width()`, and `height()` functions), and verify the expected result. If you discover mistakes in your implementation, correct them and execute the test plan again.

A CHANGE FOR THE BETTER

Step 1: Compile your implementation of the `TextWindow` class (in the file *twindow.cpp*) and the test program in the file *testwin2.cpp*. Link the resulting object files to produce an executable file.

Step 2: Check each case in the test plan for *Test 2* (`move()` function), and verify the expected result. If you discover mistakes in your implementation, correct them and execute the test plan again.

Step 3: Compile your implementation of the `TextWindow` class (in the file *twindow.cpp*) and the test program in the file *testwin3.cpp*. Link the resulting object files to produce an executable file.

Step 4: Check each case in the test plan for *Test 3* (`resize()` function), and verify the expected result. If you discover mistakes in your implementation, correct them and execute the test plan again.

Step 5: Compile your implementation of the `TextWindow` class (in the file *twindow.cpp*) and the test program in the file *testwin4.cpp*. Link the resulting object files to produce an executable file.

Step 6: Check each case in the test plan for *Test 4* (`replaceText()` function), and verify the expected result. If you discover mistakes in your implementation, correct them and execute the test plan again.

WINDOW FRAME

Step 1: Compile your implementation of the `TextWindow` class (in the file *twindow.cpp*) and the test program in the file *testwin5.cpp*. Link the resulting object files to produce an executable file.

Step 2: Check each case in the test plan for *Test 5* (`display()` function), and verify the expected result. If you discover mistakes in your implementation, correct them and execute the test plan again.

Laboratory 9: In-lab Exercise 1

USING MULTIPLE OBJECTS

Date .... Section ....

Name ....

:-)?

You are probably ready for a fun application that uses the `TextWindow` class you developed in the Prelab Application Exercises. In this exercise you create a quiz program that uses text windows to display a series of questions regarding the meaning of various smileys.

Step 1: Create a program that reads a series of question/answer pairs from a data file. After reading in a question/answer pair, your program should display the question in a text window, wait for the user to enter a carriage return, display the answer in another text window, and wait for another carriage return. Base your program on the program shell in the file *smilquiz.shl*. A sample question/answer display is shown below.

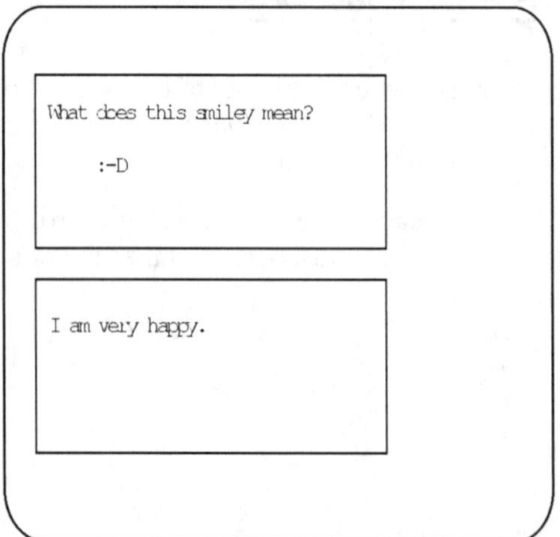

Step 2: Save your program as *smilquiz.cpp.*

Step 3: Test your program using the following test plan. If you discover mistakes in your program, correct them and execute the test plan again.

Test Plan for *smiley*			
Test case	*Sample data*	*Expected result*	*Checked*
Data file of smiley "states"	Read from file *smiley1.dat*	A series of smiley question/ answer pairs	
Data file of smiley "beings"	Read from file *smiley2.dat*	A series of smiley question/ answer pairs	

Laboratory 9: In-lab Exercise 2
APPLYING THE TextWindow CLASS

Date .... Section ....

Name ....

FORGET ME NOT

Do you find your computer monitor cluttered with reminder notes describing things that you need to do? Why not display these notes on the screen? You can create a moving window containing a reminder note using the `move()` and `display()` functions from your `TextWindow` class.

Step 1: Create a program that displays a reminder note in a moving text window on the screen. Have the reminder note move from the upper left-hand corner of the screen to the lower right-hand corner and back again. Base your program on the program shell in the file *reminder.shl.* The movements of a sample reminder note are shown below.

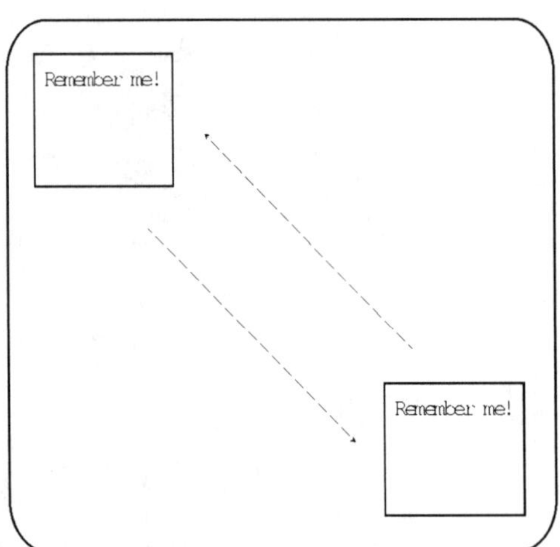

Step 2: Save your program as *reminder.cpp*.

Step 3: Test your program using the following test plan. If you discover mistakes in your program, correct them and execute the test plan again.

Test Plan for *reminder*

Test case	*Sample data*	*Expected result*	*Checked*
My note	`Remember to stop me`	Reminder note window moves from the upper left-hand corner of the screen to the lower right-hand corner and back again.	
Your note			

Laboratory 9: Postlab Exercise

DESIGNING CLASSES

Date .... Section ....

Name ....

In the Prelab and In-lab Exercises you were provided with class declarations and function specifications for the `Point` and `TextWindow` classes that you were asked to implement. In this exercise you specify the member functions and data members for a new `StopWatch` class that can be used to measure time intervals up to 60 minutes long.

PART A

Give function specifications for the member functions that form the public interface for your `StopWatch` class. Use the function specification style used in the Prelab and In-lab Exercises.

PART B

List the private data members that you would include in your `StopWatch` class. Briefly describe the information stored in each data member.

Files and Streams

OVERVIEW

In the programs that you have written thus far, you have entered data interactively from the keyboard and displayed output on the screen. In this lab you learn how to read input from a file and output results to a file. You also examine some of the functions and manipulators provided in the C++ stream libraries.

In Prelab Exercise 1, you use the `setw`, `setprecision`, and `setiosflags` stream manipulators to give you more control over how output—particularly, numeric output—is displayed. In Prelab Exercise 2, you learn how to read data from an input file and how to write data to an output file. In Prelab Exercise 3, you explore use of the `get()` and `getline()` functions to read in characters and strings, respectively.

LABORATORY 10: Cover Sheet

Date .... Section ....

Name ....

Place a checkmark in the *Assigned* column next to the exercises that your instructor has assigned to you. Have this sheet ready when your lab instructor checks your work. If your exercises are being checked outside the laboratory session, attach this sheet to the front of the packet of materials that you submit.

Exercise		*Assigned*	*Completed*
Prelab 1	Output Manipulators		
Prelab 2	File Input/Output		
Prelab 3	Get and Getline		
Bridge	Testing and Debugging the Prelab Application Exercises *Thunder and Lightning* *Statistically Speaking* *String Along*		
In-lab 1	Applying File Input/Output		
In-lab 2	Sorting		
Postlab	Analyzing Stream Processing		
		Total	

Laboratory 10: Prelab Exercise 1

OUTPUT MANIPULATORS

Date .... Section ....

Name ....

BACKGROUND

C++ output streams use a group of settings to specify how data is to be displayed by the output stream insertion operator <<. You can change these settings using the output stream **input/output manipulators** declared in the file *iomanip.h* and in this way control how your output is formatted.

Let's begin by examining the following program from the file *car1.cpp.*

```
// Calculates the total cost of a car purchase and displays the result.

#include <iostream.h>         // For cin, cout
#include <iomanip.h>          // For output manipulators

void main()
{
    int modelNum;             // Four-digit model number
    double basePrice,         // Base price of car
           taxRate,           // Tax rate
           finalPrice;        // Total cost of car

    // Prompt the user for the car purchase data.
    cout << endl << "Enter the car's 4-digit model number: ";
    cin >> modelNum;
    cout << "Enter the car's base price: ";
    cin >> basePrice;
    cout << "Enter the tax rate (as a % of 1.0): ";
    cin >> taxRate;

    // Calculate the total cost of the purchase.
    finalPrice = basePrice * (1 + taxRate);

    // Output the model number and the purchase price (w/ headings).
    cout << endl << "Model #    Final Price" << endl;
    cout << modelNum << "     " << finalPrice << endl;
}
```

The output produced by a sample run of this program is shown below:

```
Enter the car's 4-digit model number: 1234
Enter the car's base price: 9995.95
Enter the tax rate (as a % of 1.0): 0.07

Model #     Final Price
1234     10695.6665
```

This output suffers from several defects. Not only are the columns not properly aligned, but the final price is shown to four decimal places rather than two—the final price should read 10695.67. Things get even uglier if we try to price a very expensive car—a multi-million-dollar antique, for instance:

```
Enter the car's 4-digit model number: 1234
Enter the car's base price: 15000000
Enter the tax rate (as a % of 1.0): 0.15

Model #     Final Price
1234     1.725e+07
```

Not only are the columns out of alignment, but the price is displayed in scientific notation rather than the fixed-point form that most people are accustomed to using.

Let's solve the alignment problem first. You use the `setw` manipulator to specify the **field width** for the next output value—that is, the number of columns (character positions) that are reserved for displaying the value. Replacing the last `cout` statement in *car1.cpp* with

```
cout << setw(7) << modelNum << "     "
     << setw(11) << finalPrice << endl;
```

sets the field width for `modelNum` to 7 and the field width for `finalPrice` to 11. The values 7 and 11 are based on the lengths of the headings `"Model #"` and `"Final Price"`, respectively. The resulting output is shown below:

```
Enter the car's 4-digit model number: 1234
Enter the car's base price: 9995.95
Enter the tax rate (as a % of 1.0): 0.07

Model #     Final Price
   1234      10695.6665
```

Note that each value is output right-justified within its field. Note also that `setw` only changes the field width for the next value output to `cout`. After this value is output, the field width reverts to its default value.

Having addressed the alignment problem, let's look at the problem of displaying the final price in the form we want. You use the `setprecision` manipulator to specify the number of digits that should be displayed to the right of the decimal point. The call

```
setprecision(2)
```

indicates that all subsequent floating-point values should be output with two digits to the right of the decimal point. You use the `setiosflags` manipulator to specify the **formatting flags** (settings) that further control the output of floating-point values. The call

```
setiosflags( ios::fixed | ios::showpoint )
```

specifies that all subsequent floating-point values are to be displayed in fixed-point form (`ios::fixed`) and forces display of the decimal point and any trailing zeroes (`ios::showpoint`)—even if a floating-point value is a whole number. Note that unlike `setw`, the settings specified by the `setprecision` and `setiosflags` manipulators remain in effect until they are explicitly changed by another call to `setprecision` or `setiosflags`.

Replacing the last `cout` statement in *car1.cpp* with

```
cout << setprecision(2)
     << setiosflags( ios::fixed | ios::showpoint )
     << setw(7) << modelNum << "     "
     << setw(11) << finalPrice << endl;
```

produces the following sets of output for base prices of 9995.95 and 15,000,000, respectively:

```
Enter the car's 4-digit model number: 1234
Enter the car's base price: 9995.95
Enter the tax rate (as a % of 1.0): 0.07

Model #     Final Price
   1234        10695.67


Enter the car's 4-digit model number: 1234
Enter the car's base price: 15000000
Enter the tax rate (as a % of 1.0): 0.15

Model #     Final Price
   1234     17250000.00
```

WARM-UP EXERCISE

Complete the following program by filling in the missing C++ code. A shell for this program is given in the file *sales1.shl.*

```
// Calculates an employee's sales commission and displays the result
// using formatted output.

#include <iostream.h>          // For cin, cout
#include ____________          // For output manipulators

void main()
{
    int IDNum;                 // Four-digit employee ID number
    double totalSales,         // Total sales
           commissionRate,     // Commission rate
           commission;         // Employee's sales commission

    // Prompt the user for the employee data.
    cout << endl << "Enter the employee's four-digit ID number: ";
    cin >> IDNum;
    cout << "Enter the employee's total sales: ";
    cin >> totalSales;
    cout << "Enter the commission rate (as a % of 1.0): ";
    cin >> commissionRate;

    // Calculate the employee's sales commission.
    commission = commissionRate * totalSales;

    // Output the employee ID and commission earned (w/ headings).



}
```

THUNDER AND LIGHTNING

You can compute a rough estimate of your distance (in miles) from a lightning strike by counting the number of seconds between the lightning flash and the thunder clap, and dividing the result by 5. In this exercise you explore the basis for this estimation technique by comparing how long it takes the lightning flash to reach you with how long it takes the sound of the thunder clap to reach you.

You can compute the length of time that it takes light to cover a given distance using the formula

$$Time_{light} = \frac{distance}{speed\ of\ light}$$

where $time_{light}$ is measured in seconds, *distance* is measured in miles, and the *speed of light* is 186,000 miles per second. Similarly, you can compute the length of time that it takes sound to cover a given distance using the formula

$$Time_{sound} = \frac{distance}{speed\ of\ sound}$$

where $time_{sound}$ is measured in seconds, *distance* is measured in miles, and the *speed of sound* is 0.206 miles per second (that is, one-fifth of a mile per second).

Step 1: Create a program that computes the length of time that it takes light and sound to cover a given distance. The time for light should be displayed using scientific notation, while the time for sound should be displayed in fixed-point form with two decimal places to the right of the decimal point.

Input: Distance (in miles)

Output: Columns showing the distance (in miles), the length of time that it takes light to travel this distance, and the length of time that it takes sound to travel this distance (both times are in seconds)

Step 2: Save your program as *thunder.cpp.*

Step 3: Complete the following test plan.

Test Plan for *thunder*			
Test case	*Sample data*	*Expected result*	*Checked*
One mile	1	Distance (miles) 1 / Time for light (seconds) 5.376e-06 / Time for sound (seconds) 4.85	
Five miles	5	Distance (miles) 5 / Time for light (seconds) 2.688e-05 / Time for sound (seconds) 24.27	

Laboratory 10: Prelab Exercise 2

FILE INPUT/OUTPUT

Date .... Section ....

Name ....

BACKGROUND

Thus far your programs have used the `cin` stream to read data from the keyboard and the `cout` stream to display output to the screen. Many programs, however, require large amounts of input data and produce results that need to be recorded for future reference—either by you or by another program. For these applications, you need to be able to read data from a file and output data to a file. C++ provides support for file input/output in the *fstream* library.

You read data from a file using an **input file stream** (or **`ifstream`**). The following statement opens the file *values.dat* for input by associating it with an input file stream object named `inFile`.

```
ifstream inFile("values.dat");
```

You read data from the file by applying the extraction operator (>>) to input file stream `inFile`. The code fragment

```
ifstream inFile("values.dat");
int num1;
inFile >> num1;
```

reads an integer value from input file *values.dat* and stores it in `num1`. Note how similar this process is to reading data from the `cin` input stream. The program *fileio1.cpp* reads five integer values from the file *values.dat* and displays their sum on the screen:

```
#include <iostream.h>  // For cin, cout
#include <fstream.h>   // For file input/output

void main()
{
    ifstream inFile("values.dat");      // Open input file values.dat
    int num,                            // Number read from file
        sum = 0;                        // Sum of numbers read in

    // Read in numbers and compute their sum.
    for ( int j = 0 ; j < 5 ; j++ )
    {
        inFile >> num;
        sum += num;
    }

    // Output the sum.
    cout << "Sum = " << sum << endl;

    // Close the input file stream.
    inFile.close();
}
```

When the input process is complete, the program closes the input file stream (and the associated file) using the `close()` function. Note that you must include the header file *fstream.h* in any program that uses input/output file streams.

Many times, you do not know how many values are stored in a file. You handle this situation by using the fact that the extraction operator actually returns a value. The call

```
inFile >> num
```

returns the value 1 if it succeeds in reading in a number from `inFile` (a number that it stores in `num`) and the value 0 if it fails. One situation in which the extraction operator fails to read in a number is when it reaches the end of a file. The following code fragment uses the value returned by the extraction operator to control a loop that reads in (and sums) all the numbers stored in a file:

```
// Read in a set of numbers. Stop when the end of the file is reached.
while ( inFile >> num )
    sum += num;
```

Many implementations of C++ produce different results depending on whether the end-of-file marker is placed at the end of a line of data or on a line by itself. You can avoid this problem by checking the status of an input stream before reading in a data value. You check a stream's status using the `good()` function as follows:

```
// Read in a set of numbers. Stop when the end of the file is reached.
while ( inFile.good()  &&  inFile >> num )
    sum += num;
```

This extra check may seem to be overkill. However, it will help to ensure that your programs run properly on a variety of systems.

Once you have seen how file input works, file output seems obvious. You open the file *results.dat* for output by associating it with an **output file stream** (or **`ofstream`**) object

```
ofstream outFile("results.dat");
```

and write data to the file by applying the insertion operator (<<) to output file stream `outFile`, as in the following example:

```
outFile << "The sum is " << sum << endl;
```

One last note regarding file input/output. It is good programming practice to confirm that a file has been opened successfully before using it. The following code from the program *fileio2.cpp*

```
void main()
{
    ifstream inFile("values.dat");

    if ( !inFile )
       cout << "values.dat could not be opened for input" << endl;
    else
    {
       ... Read the data stored in the file and output the sum ...
    }
}
```

tests whether the file *values.dat* has been opened for input. If it has not—if the file does not exist, for instance—then the program outputs an error message and terminates. Otherwise, it processes the data stored in the file.

WARM-UP EXERCISE

Complete the following program by filling in the missing C++ code. A shell for this program is given in the file *sales2.shl.*

```
// Reads sales data for an employee from a file and outputs the
// employee's total sales and sales commission to a file.

#include <iostream.h>
#include <fstream.h>     // For file input/output

void main()
{
    double saleAmount,           // Individual sale
           totalSales = 0.0,     // Total sales
           commissionRate,       // Commission rate
           commission;           // Employee commission

    // Read in the commission rate from the keyboard.
    cout << "Enter the commission rate (as a % of 1.0): ";
    cin >> commissionRate;

    // Open the file sales.dat and associate it with an input file
    // stream named salesData.
    ________________________________________

    // Test to ensure that the file opening process was successful.
    if ( ______________ )
       cout << "File sales.dat could not be opened" << endl;
    else
    {
       // Read in sales data until the end of the file is reached.
       while ( _________________________________ )
             totalSales += saleAmount;

       // Close the input file.
       ________________________

       // Calculate the employee's sales commission.
       commission = commissionRate * totalSales;

       // Open the file commiss.out and associate it with an output
       // file stream named commOut.
       ________________________________________

       // Test to ensure that the file opening process was successful.
       if ( ______________ )
          cout << "File commiss.out could not be opened" << endl;
       else
       {
          // Output the total sales and the commission to commiss.out.
          ____________ << "Total sales: $" << totalSales << endl
          ____________ << "Commission:  $" << commission << endl;

          // Close the output file.
          __________________________________
       }
    }
}
```

STATISTICALLY SPEAKING

The standard deviation is a common measurement of the spread or dispersion of data. This statistic gives an indication of how individual data items are scattered about the mean (average) of a sample data set. Formulas for computing the mean ($\bar{x}$) and standard deviation (s) of a set of data values $x_1, x_2, \ldots, x_n$ are given below:

$$\bar{x} = \sum_{i=1}^{n} x_i \qquad s^2 = \frac{\sum_{i=1}^{n} \left(x_i - \bar{x}\right)^2}{n-1} = \frac{\left(\sum_{i=1}^{n} x_i^2\right) - n \cdot \bar{x}^2}{n-1}$$

Applying these formulas to the following 10 values

20 14 23 16 15 18 12 20 22 17

yields a mean of 17.7 and a standard deviation of 3.56.

Step 1: Create a program that computes the mean and standard deviation for a set of floating-point values in an input file. The resulting mean and standard deviation should be output to the file *stats.out.*

Input: A set of floating-point values in a file

Output: The mean and standard deviation of the input values are output to the file *stats.out*

Step 2: Save your program as *stats.cpp.*

Step 3: Complete the following test plan.

Test Plan for *stats*			
Test case	*Sample data*	*Expected result*	*Checked*
Large range of values in data set	*vals1.dat*	Mean: 4.0 Std. dev.: 1.58	
Small range of values in data set	*vals2.dat*	Mean: 17.7 Std. dev.: 3.56	

Laboratory 10: Prelab Exercise 3

GET AND GETLINE

Date .... Section ....

Name ....

BACKGROUND

When reading in individual characters, the extraction operator (>>) ignores any whitespace (spaces, tabs, and newline markers) that it encounters in an input stream. The statement

```
cin >> ch1 >> ch2;
```

for instance, reads two characters from the `cin` input stream. Whether the input is

```
ab
```

or

```
a b
```

or

```
a
b
```

the result is the same: `'a'` is assigned to `ch1` and `'b'` is assigned to `ch2`.

Sometimes the whitespace in an input stream is significant and should not be ignored. C++ provides the `get()` function for just such situations. The `get()` function reads the next character from the input stream, even if the character is a whitespace character. The following code fragment reads two characters from the `cin` input stream:

```
cin.get(ch1);
cin.get(ch2);
```

When the input is

```
ab
```

the result produced matches that produced by the extraction operator: `'a'` is assigned to `ch1` and `'b'` is assigned to `ch2`. When the input is

```
a b
```

however, the results are different: `'a'` is assigned to `ch1` and `' '` (a space) is assigned to `ch2`—the `'b'` is left in the input stream for later processing. Attempting to enter the characters one per line produces an even more marked difference: `'a'` is assigned to `ch1` and `'\n'` (the newline marker) is assigned to `ch2`—you are not even given the chance to enter `'b'`.

Often you use the `get()` function simply to skip a space or a newline marker. In this case, you can use `get()` without an argument:

```
cin.get();
```

The character read from the input stream is discarded.

Whitespace presents a different problem when it comes to reading in strings. The extraction operator treats whitespace as a string delimiter. This approach is fine when you are reading in a pair of names or a series of commands. It causes problems, however, when the string you are attempting to read contains spaces—a sentence or a phrase, for instance. Fortunately, C++ provides a function, `getline()`, that reads a sequence of characters—including whitespace—from an input stream.

The `getline()` function has three parameters:

```
getline ( char dest[], int size, char delimiter )
```

The first parameter is the character array (string) that returns the characters read from in the input stream. The second parameter is the size of the array. The final parameter is the character that marks the end of the string in the input stream—the string delimiter. The `getline()` function reads characters from the input stream until either it has read `size-1` characters or the `delimiter` character is encountered. In either case, the `getline()` function appends the null character (`'\0'`) to the string. Note that if the delimiter is encountered, it is not placed in the string. Instead, it is removed from the input stream and discarded.

The following code fragment uses `getline()` to read a sentence from the keyboard:

```
const int STR_LENGTH = 11;
char textString[STR_LENGTH];
cout << endl << "Enter a sentence: " << endl;
cin.getline(textString,STR_LENGTH,'\n');
```

The sentence

```
Hi there!
```

for example, produces the following `textString`:

textString[0]	'H'
textString[1]	'i'
textString[2]	' '
textString[3]	't'
textString[4]	'h'
textString[5]	'e'
textString[6]	'r'
textString[7]	'e'
textString[8]	'!'
textString[9]	'\0'
textString[10]	

In this case, the `getline()` function stopped reading characters when it encountered the newline marker.

WARM-UP EXERCISE

A list of files often includes a short description of each file. A common format for file descriptions is

filename description

where each filename is followed by a short description of the file's contents or purpose. Note that the name and description are separated by two spaces, as in

```
mainfile.cpp  Driver program for the project
```

Complete the following program by filling in the missing C++ code. A shell for this program is given in the file *filelist.shl.*

```
// Reads in a file name followed by a short description of the file's
// contents.

#include <iostream.h>

void main ()
{
    char filename[13],
         description[41];

    cout << endl << "Enter a filename followed by a description "
         << "of its contents:" << endl;

    // Read in the name of the file.
    ________________________________

    // Read in the two spaces.


    // Read in the description of the file.
    ____________________________________________

    cout << endl << "File: " << filename << endl
         << "Description: " << description << endl;
}
```

STRING ALONG

Suppose that you wish to read in a pair of file descriptions, one per line, using the `getline()` function. At first glance, this might appear to be an easy task—the code fragment below would seem to do the job quite well:

```
const int DESCRIP_LEN = 41;
char descrip1[DESCRIP_LEN],
     descrip2[DESCRIP_LEN];

cout << "Enter a pair of file descriptions:" << endl;
cin.getline(descrip1,DESCRIP_LEN,'\n');
cin.getline(descrip2,DESCRIP_LEN,'\n');
```

Unfortunately, in this case, looks are deceiving. Consider what happens when the following file descriptions are input from the keyboard:

```
This description is more than 40 characters long
A shorter description
```

The first call to `getline()` returns the string

```
This description is more than 40 charact
```

while the second call returns the string

```
ers long
```

Rather than reading two file descriptions, we have read the first description in two parts. A more aggravating result is produced by the following input descriptions:

```
This description is exactly 40 char long
A shorter description
```

In this case, the first call to `getline()` returns the string

```
This description is exactly 40 char long
```

while the second call returns the empty string—that is, the null character alone. The problem here is that the first call to `getline()` stopped reading when the size limit was reached, leaving the newline marker in the input stream. The second call read this marker and stopped immediately. This result is more frustrating because the first file description fits within the 40-character limit specified by the constant `DESCRIP_LEN`.

The following variation of the `getline()` function addresses these problems by always reading until the delimiter is encountered:

`void getlineDelim ( char dest[], int size, char delimiter )`

Input parameters
`size:` size of the `dest` array
`delimiter:` string delimiter in the input stream

Output parameter
`dest[]:` string read from the input stream. Function reads characters from the input stream until either it has read `size-1` characters or the `delimiter` character is encountered. If the size limit stops the reading process, then the function continues reading until the delimiter is encountered—the extra characters read in are discarded. In either case, the function appends the null character (`'\0'`) to the string.

Step 1: Create the function `getlineDelim()` specified above.

Step 2: Add your `getlineDelim()` function to the file *testget.cpp*.

Step 3: Complete the following test plan. The following test cases assume that the `size` argument is 11.

Test Plan for getlineDelim()

Test case	*Sample data*	*Expected result*	*Checked*
Input strings contain less than 10 characters	`String 1` `String 2`	String 1 String 2	
First input string contains more than 10 characters	`Too many characters` `String 2`	Too many c String 2	
First input string contains exactly 10 characters	`Ten string` `String 2`	Ten string String 2	
Both input strings contain more than 10 characters	`Long string` `Longer string`	Long strin Longer str	

Laboratory 10: Bridge Exercise

TESTING AND DEBUGGING THE PRELAB APPLICATION EXERCISES

Date .... Section ....

Name ....

Check with your instructor whether you need to complete this exercise before your lab session or during lab.

THUNDER AND LIGHTNING

Step 1: Execute your program in the file *thunder.cpp.*

Step 2: Check each case in your *thunder* test plan, and verify the expected result. If you discover mistakes in your program, correct them and execute the test plan again.

STATISTICALLY SPEAKING

Step 1: Execute your program in the file *stats.cpp.*

Step 2: Check each case in your *stats* test plan, and verify the expected result. If you discover mistakes in your program, correct them and execute the test plan again.

STRING ALONG

Step 1: Execute the program in the file *testget.cpp.*

Step 2: Check each case in your *getlineDelim()* test plan, and verify the expected result. If you discover mistakes in your function, correct them and execute the test plan again.

Laboratory 10: In-lab Exercise 1

APPLYING FILE INPUT/OUTPUT

Date .... Section ....

Name ....

BEHIND BARS

Universal Product Codes (UPCs) appear on almost everything we buy. If you look closely at a UPC bar code, you will see a sequence of numbers. These numbers are included so that humans can identify a product. For many—but not all—products, there are two five-digit numbers, one designating the product manufacturer and one designating the product item. The codes from a can of Campbell's Chicken Noodle Soup are shown below:

```
    51000           01251
Manufacturer       Product
```

In this exercise you create a program that reads information on a series of products from an input file, identifies the products made by a specific manufacturer, and saves the information about these products to another file. The input file consists of product data in the following form:

manufacturer product description

where *manufacturer* and *product* are the UPC numbers identifying a product and *description* is a product description.

Your program should begin by asking the user for the following information: the name of the input file to process, the manufacturer's five-digit code, and the name of the output file to create. After opening both files, it should read through the input file line-by-line (product-by-product). Whenever it reads in a product made by the specified manufacturer, it should output the product information (UPC numbers and description) to the output file.

Step 1: Create the program described above.

Input: The name of the input file to process
A manufacturer's five-digit code
The name of the output file to create

Output: Information on the products made by the specified manufacturer is output to the output file

Step 2: Save your program as *upc.cpp.*

Step 3: Test your program using the following test plan. If you discover mistakes in your program, correct them and execute the test plan again.

Test Plan for *upc*			
Test case	*Data file*	*Expected result*	*Checked*
Select the products made by Quaker Oats (30000) and save them in the file *quaker.dat*	*grocery.dat*	30000 1200 Quaker Quick Oats 30000 3050 Quaker Corn Meal 30000 2190 Kretschmer Wheat Germ	
Select the products made by Campbell's Soup (51000) and save them in the file *campbell.dat*	*grocery.dat*	51000 1251 Campbell's Chicken Noodle Soup 51000 5977 Campbell's Healthy Cream of Chicken 51000 2548 Prego Traditional Spaghetti Sauce	

Laboratory 10: In-lab Exercise 2

SORTING

Date .... Section ....

Name ....

LONG DISTANCE

Finding a number in a sorted list is much easier than finding a number in an unsorted list, especially if the list is long. There are many ways to sort a list. In this exercise you use an intuitive—if somewhat inefficient—sorting algorithm called a **selection sort**.

Suppose that you are given the following unsorted array of integers:

Array index	0	1	2	3	4	5	6	7	8	9
Array entry	24	57	71	89	23	46	35	15	42	63

and are asked to sort the integers into ascending order (from smallest to largest). You begin a selection sort by locating the smallest integer value in the array. You locate this value using a loop in which you examine each array entry (`k`) while keeping track of the location where the smallest value found thus far is located (`minPos`):

```
minPos = 0;
for ( k = 1 ; k < size ; k++ )
    if ( list[k] < list[minPos] )
       minPos = k;
```

After checking the entire array, `minPos` is 7, indicating that array entry 7 contains the smallest value in the array:

Array index	0	1	2	3	4	5	6	7	8	9
Array entry	24	57	71	89	23	46	35	15	42	63
								↑ minPos		

Once you have located the smallest value, you exchange this value with the first element in the array (the element with index 0):

Array index	0	1	2	3	4	5	6	7	8	9
Array entry	15	57	71	89	23	46	35	24	42	63

Having positioned the smallest value in its correct location in the sorted array, you continue sorting by locating the next-to-smallest value. Note that you only need to search array entries 1 to 9:

Array index	0	1	2	3	4	5	6	7	8	9
Array entry	15	57	71	89	23	46	35	24	42	63
					↑ minPos					

You then exchange the next-to-smallest value with the second element in the array (the element with index 1):

Array index	0	1	2	3	4	5	6	7	8	9
Array entry	15	23	71	89	57	46	35	24	42	63

Repeating this process seven more times (with increasingly smaller subsets of the array) yields a sorted array:

Array index	0	1	2	3	4	5	6	7	8	9
Array entry	15	23	24	35	42	46	57	63	71	89

An implementation of the selection sort algorithm is given below.

```
void selectionSort ( int list[], int size )

// Selection sort routine. Sorts the list into ascending order.
// Parameter size is the number of integers in the list.

{
    int temp,       // Temporary storage used in swapping
        minPos,     // Index of smallest value among remaining entries
        j,          // Outer loop counter
        k;          // Inner loop (min search) counter

    for ( j = 0 ; j < size-1 ; j++ )
    {
        minPos = j;                            // Find smallest value
        for ( k = j+1 ; k < size ; k++ )       // in remainder of array
            if ( list[k] < list[minPos] )
               minPos = k;
        temp          = list[j];               // Exchange
        list[j]       = list[minPos];
        list[minPos] = temp;
    }
}
```

Step 1: Create a program that reads a set of pairs (area code, city name) from the file *areacode.dat* into an array, sorts the array in ascending order based on area code, and outputs the sorted array to the file *acsorted.dat*. Base your program on the program shell given in the file *sortarea.shl*.

Step 2: Test your program using the following test plan. If you discover mistakes in your program, correct them and execute the test plan again.

Test Plan for *sortarea*			
Test case	*Data file*	*Expected result*	*Checked*
Sort the area code list in the file *areacode.dat* and store the sorted list in the file *acsorted.dat*	*areacode.dat*	Sorted list in the file *acsorted.dat*	

Laboratory 10: Postlab Exercise

ANALYZING STREAM PROCESSING

Date .... Section ....

Name ....

PART A

The following program from the file *sumscore.cpp* is designed to sum a set of scores:

```
#include <iostream.h>
#include <fstream.h>

void main ()
{
    int score,
        sum = 0;

    ifstream inFile("scores.dat");

    while ( inFile >> score )
        sum += score;

    inFile.close();

    cout << "The sum is " << sum << endl;
}
```

Explain why this program produces an incorrect sum for the scores in the data file *scores.dat*.

PART B

Describe the output produced by the following program from the file *mystery.cpp.* What output do the characters '\t', '\n', and '\a' produce?

```
#include <iostream.h>
#include <math.h>

void main ()
{
    cout << "Number\tSquare Root";

    for ( int j = 5; j >= 1; j-- )
        cout << '\n'<< j << '\t' << sqrt(j);

    cout << "\nHit <RETURN> to continue\n";
    cin.get();
    cout << "\a\n";
}
```

Functions II

OVERVIEW

You created two types of functions in Laboratory 6—functions that return a single value and void functions. In this lab you expand your knowledge of the range of features supported by C++ functions. You also experiment with a new style of programming based on recursive functions—that is, functions that call themselves.

In Prelab Exercise 1, you use pass-by-reference to create functions that return multiple values. In Prelab Exercise 2, you explore how the use of function overloading allows you to give the same name to several functions that perform similar tasks but which differ in the number of arguments or types of arguments they process. Prelab Exercise 3 is an exploration of recursive functions—how to create them and how to use them.

LABORATORY 11: Cover Sheet

Date .... Section ....

Name ....

Place a checkmark in the *Assigned* column next to the exercises that your instructor has assigned to you. Have this sheet ready when your lab instructor checks your work. If your exercises are being checked outside the laboratory session, attach this sheet to the front of the packet of materials that you submit.

Exercise		*Assigned*	*Completed*
Prelab 1	Pass-by-Reference		
Prelab 2	Overloading		
Prelab 3	Recursion		
Bridge	Testing and Debugging the Prelab Application Exercises *Painting the Town* *Boxed In* *Prestidigitation*		
In-lab 1	Applying Pass-by-Reference		
In-lab 2	Applying Recursion		
Postlab	Potential Pitfalls Using Overloading and Recursion		
		Total	

Laboratory 11: Prelab Exercise 1

PASS-BY-REFERENCE

Date .... Section ....

Name ....

BACKGROUND

Sometimes you need to return more than a single value from a function—when a function computes a set of results, for instance. One way to return multiple values from a function is to pass the results back to the calling routine using the arguments in the function call. The following call

```
rectangleProperties(length,width,area,perimeter);
```

passes the length and width of a rectangle to the function `rectangleProperties()` and returns with arguments `area` and `perimeter` containing the rectangle's area and perimeter, respectively.

The argument-passing mechanism you used in Lab 6 does not allow you to change an argument's value in this way. This mechanism, called **pass-by-value**, copies an argument's value and passes the copy to the function via the corresponding function parameter. Any changes made to the parameter within the function affect only the parameter, not the original argument.

Fortunately, C++ provides another argument-passing mechanism, called **pass-by-reference**, in which the address in memory where an argument is stored is passed to a function. As a result, changes made to the corresponding parameter change the argument also. The following program from the file *params.cpp* demonstrates how to return information using pass-by-reference.

```
// Comparing pass-by-value and pass-by-reference.

#include <iostream.h>

void paramFun ( int &x, int &y, int z );   // x and y are reference
                                           // parameters
void main()
{
    int a = 1,
        b = 3,
        c = 4;

    cout << "In main(), before call to paramFun()" << endl;
    cout << "a:" << a << " b:" << b << " c:" << c;
    cout << endl << endl;
    paramFun(a,b,c);
    cout << "In main(), after call to paramFun()" << endl;
```

```
    cout << "a:" << a << " b:" << b << " c:" << c;
    cout << endl << endl;
}

void paramFun ( int &x, int &y, int z )
{
    x++;
    y += 2;
    z *= 3;
    cout << "Inside paramFun()" << endl;
    cout << "x:" << x << " y:" << y << " z:" << z;
    cout << endl << endl;
}
```

Variables a and b in `main()` are passed to parameters x and y in function `paramFun()` using pass-by-reference. You designate a parameter as a **reference parameter** by placing an ampersand (`&`) between the parameter type and the parameter name. The prototype for `paramFun()`

```
void paramFun ( int &x, int &y, int z );
```

indicates that x and y are reference parameters. Note that parameters x and y are actually nothing more than aliases for variables a and b in `main()`. Thus any changes that are made to x and y in `paramFun()` are actually made to a and b. The use of pass-by-reference is reflected in the following sample output:

```
In main(), before call to paramFun()
a:1 b:3 c:4

Inside paramFun()
x:2 y:5 z:12

In main(), after call to paramFun()
a:2 b:5 c:4
```

Parameter z, on the other hand, is a **value parameter**—a copy of argument c is passed to `paramFun()`, not the address of argument c. As a result, changing the value of z to 12 has no impact on argument c—it remains 4.

Reference parameters provide a form of two-way communication between functions. Value parameters, on the other hand, only allow information to be communicated one way—into a function. In our function specifications we will categorize parameters as follows: any parameter that carries information into a function is an **input parameter**, any parameter that returns results from a function is an **output parameter**, and any parameter that does both is an **input/output parameter**. Input parameters can be either value or reference parameters. Output and input/output parameters must be reference parameters, however.

WARM-UP EXERCISE

You frequently need to exchange the values of two variables in your programs. The function `swap()` specified below uses a pair of reference parameters to exchange two integers:

void swap (int &x, int &y)

Input/output parameters

x, y: (input) two integers
(output) the integers exchanged

Complete the following program by filling in the missing C++ code. A shell for this program is given in the file *swapref.shl*.

```
// Exchanges the values of two integer variables using the pass-by-
// reference mechanism.

#include <iostream.h>

void swap ( ______________________ );    // Prototype

void main ()
{
    int a, b;

    cout << endl << "Enter two integers separated by a space: ";
    cin >> a >> b;
    cout << "Before swap" << endl;
    cout << "a:" << a << " b:" << b << endl << endl;

    // Exchange the values of a and b.
    ________________________________________
    cout << "After swap" << endl;
    cout << "a:" << a << " b:" << b << endl;
}

void swap ( ________________________________ )
// Exchanges the integers.
{
    _______________
    _______________
    _______________
    _______________
}
```

PAINTING THE TOWN

Before painting a room, you need to estimate how many gallons of paint you need to purchase to complete the job. Things to consider when making your estimate include the dimensions of the room, the number of windows and doors in the room, whether you are painting the ceiling in addition to the walls, and how many coats of paint you intend to apply.

Preparing your estimate is easier if you use a few "painter's rules of thumb":

- One gallon of paint covers approximately 400 square feet of smooth, well-prepared surface with one coat of paint.
- The area of the average window is 15 square feet.
- The area of the average door is 21 square feet.

Step 1: Create a function `paintEstimate()` that computes the number of gallons of paint needed to paint the walls and ceiling of a rectangular room. Base your function on the following specification:

```
void paintEstimate ( double length, double width,
                     double height, int windows, int doors,
                     double &wallGals, double &ceilingGals  )
```

Input parameters
`length, width, height:` room dimensions (in feet)
`windows, doors:` numbers of windows and doors

Output parameters
`wallGals:` amount of paint needed for the walls (in gallons)
`ceilingGals:` amount of paint needed for the ceiling (in gallons)

Assume that you are applying one coat of paint to the walls and ceiling and that you are not painting the doors and windows.

Step 2: Add your `paintEstimate()` function to the test program in the file *testpnt.cpp*.

Step 3: Complete the following test plan.

Test Plan for *paintEstimate()*			
Test case	*Sample data*	*Expected result*	*Checked*
Small room			
Length: 12 feet	12	Paint needed for walls: 0.72 gallon	
Width: 8 feet	8	Paint needed for ceiling: 0.24 gallon	
Height: 9 feet	9		
Number of windows: 2	2		
Number of doors: 2	2		
Large room			
Length: 25 feet	25	Paint needed for walls: 2.445 gallons	
Width: 20 feet	20	Paint needed for ceiling: 1.25 gallons	
Height: 12 feet	12		
Number of windows: 4	4		
Number of doors: 2	2		
Medium room			

Laboratory 11: Prelab Exercise 2

OVERLOADING

Date .... Section ....

Name ....

BACKGROUND

As you begin to create a wider range of programs, you frequently find yourself creating functions that perform essentially the same task but which have different numbers of parameters or different types of parameters. You might, for example, need a function that returns the smaller of two characters (based on their ASCII codes) and another function that returns the smaller of two double-precision values. You could name the first function `minCharacter()` and the second function `minDouble()`, but it would be more convenient to give both functions the same name. C++ allows you to assign the same name to several functions—provided the functions differ in the number or type of parameters—a feature called **function overloading**.

The following excerpt from the program *minover.cpp* uses the overloaded function `min()` to determine the smaller of two characters and two double-precision numbers.

```
// Demonstrates function overloading

#include <iostream.h>

// Prototypes for two parameter functions
char min ( char x, char y );          // Char parameters
double min ( double x, double y );    // Double parameters
...

void main ()
{
    // Call min() with two character arguments.
    cout << endl << min('A','B') << " has the smaller ASCII value"
         << endl;

    // Call min() with two double-precision arguments.
    cout << min(10.5,20.0) << " is the smaller number" << endl;
    ...
}

//--------------------------------------------------------------------

char min ( char x, char y )
// Returns the character with the smaller ASCII value.
{
    char result;    // Result returned
```

```
    if ( x < y )
       result = x;
    else
       result = y;
    return result;
}

//-------------------------------------------------------------------

double min ( double x, double y )
// Returns the smaller of two double-precision values.
{
    double result;    // Result returned
    if ( x < y )
       result = x;
    else
       result = y;
    return result;
}
...
```

This excerpt produces the following output:

```
A has the smaller ASCII value
10.5 is the smaller number
```

The compiler selects the appropriate `min()` function based on the data type of the arguments in the function call. When the call

```
min('A','B')
```

is executed in `main()`, for instance, the function

```
char min ( char x, char y )
```

is invoked because the call contains arguments of type `char`.

You also can overload functions based on the number of parameters they process. The following excerpt from *minover.cpp* uses the overloaded `min()` function to find the minimum of two or three double-precision values.

```
// Demonstrates function overloading

#include <iostream.h>

// Prototypes for two parameter functions
double min ( double x, double y );            // Double parameters
...
// Prototypes for three parameter functions
double min ( double x, double y, double z );  // Double parameters
...
```

```
void main ()
{
    ...
    // Call min() with two double-precision arguments.
    cout << min(10.5,20.0) << " is the smaller number" << endl;

    ...
    // Call min() with three double-precision arguments.
    cout << min(10.5,20.0,5.5) << " is the smallest number" << endl;
}
...

//----------------------------------------------------------------------

double min ( double x, double y )
// Returns the smaller of three double-precision values.
{
    double result;    // Result returned
    if ( x < y )
       result = x;
    else
       result = y;
    return result;
}
...

//----------------------------------------------------------------------

double min ( double x, double y, double z )

// Returns the smallest of three double-precision values.
{
    double result;    // Result returned
    if ( x < y )
       if ( x < z )
          result = x;
       else
          result = z;
    else
       if ( y < z )
          result = y;
       else
          result = z;
    return result;
}
```

In this case, the compiler invokes the appropriate `min()` function based on the number of arguments in the function call. For example, the call

```
min(10.5,20.0,5.5)
```

invokes the function

```
double min ( double x, double y, double z )
```

because the call contains three arguments of type `double`.

WARM-UP EXERCISE

In this exercise you overload the `swap()` function from the first Warm-up Exercise so that you can use it to exchange characters as well as integers.

`void swap ( int &x, int &y )`
Input/output parameters
`x, y:` (input) two integers
(output) the integers exchanged

`void swap ( char &x, char &y )`
Input/output parameters
`x, y:` (input) two characters
(output) the characters exchanged

Complete the following program by filling in the missing C++ code. A shell for this program is given in the file *swapover.shl.*

```
#include <iostream.h>

void swap ( ________________________ );    // Two char parameters
void swap ( ________________________ );    // Two integer parameters

void main ()
{
    char a, b;
    int c, d;

    cout << endl << "Enter a two-letter word: ";
    cin >> a >> b;

    // Exchange two characters.
    swap(a,b);
    cout << a << b << endl;

    cout << "Enter two numbers: ";
    cin >> c >> d;

    // Exchange two integers.
    swap(c,d);
    cout << c << ' ' << d << endl;
}

//-----------------------------------------------------------------

void swap ( ______________________________ )
// Exchanges two characters.
{
    ____________
    ____________
    ____________
    ____________
}
```

```
//-----------------------------------------------------------------

void swap ( ______________________________ )
// Exchanges two integers.
{
    ____________
    ____________
    ____________
    ____________
}
```

BOXED IN

In this exercise you create an overloaded function `displayBox()` that displays a rectangular box. You overload `displayBox()` based on both the type and the number of parameters. The specifications for the `displayBox()` functions are given below:

`void displayBox ( int length )`

Input parameter
`length`: length of the sides of the box

Outputs
Displays the specified box.

`void displayBox ( int length, char fillChar )`

Input parameters
`length`: length of the sides of the box
`fillChar`: character to fill the box with

Outputs
Displays the specified box and fills it with repetitions of `fillChar`.

`void displayBox ( int width, int height )`

Input parameters
`width`: width of the box
`height`: height of the box

Outputs
Displays the specified box.

`void displayBox ( int width, int height, char fillChar )`

Input parameters
`width`: width of the box
`height`: height of the box
`fillChar`: character to fill the box with

Outputs
Displays the specified box and fills it with repetitions of `fillChar`.

Step 1: Create the overloaded function `displayBox()` specified above. Form the top and bottom of the box using the character `'-'` and the sides using `'|'`. The box displayed by the call `displayBox(15,5,'a')` is shown below:

```
---------------
|aaaaaaaaaaaaa|
|aaaaaaaaaaaaa|
|aaaaaaaaaaaaa|
---------------
```

If your system supports an extended character set, feel free to create continuous borders rather than the dashed borders shown above.

Step 2: Add your `displayBox()` functions to the test program in the file *testbox.cpp*.

Step 3: Complete the following test plan.

Test Plan for *displayBox()*

Test case	*Sample data*	*Expected result*	*Checked*

Length of sides = 5	5	`-----`
		`|   |`
		`|   |`
		`|   |`
		`-----`	

Fill box above with '?'	?	`-----`
		`|???|`
		`|???|`
		`|???|`
		`-----`	

Width = 15, height = 4	15 4	`---------------`
		`|             |`
		`|             |`
		`---------------`	

Fill box above with '$'	$		

Laboratory 11: Prelab Exercise 3

RECURSION

Date .... Section ....

Name ....

BACKGROUND

Recursive functions—that is, functions that call themselves—provide an elegant way of describing and implementing solutions to a wide range of problems, including problems in mathematics, computer graphics, compiler design, and artificial intelligence. Let's begin by examining how you develop a recursive function definition using the factorial function as an example.

You can express the factorial of a positive integer n using the following iterative formula:

$$n! = n \cdot (n-1) \cdot (n-2) \cdot \ldots \cdot 1$$

Applying this formula to 4! yields the product $4 \cdot 3 \cdot 2 \cdot 1$. If you regroup the terms in this product as $4 \cdot (3 \cdot 2 \cdot 1)$ and note that $3! = 3 \cdot 2 \cdot 1$, then you find that 4! can be written as $4 \cdot (3!)$. You can generalize this reasoning to form the following recursive definition of factorial:

$$n! = n \cdot (n-1)!$$

where 0! is defined to be 1. Applying this definition to the evaluation of 4! yields the following sequence of computations:

$$\begin{aligned} 4! &= 4 \cdot (3!) \\ &= 4 \cdot (3 \cdot (2!)) \\ &= 4 \cdot (3 \cdot (2 \cdot (1!))) \\ &= 4 \cdot (3 \cdot (2 \cdot (1 \cdot (0!)))) \\ &= 4 \cdot (3 \cdot (2 \cdot (1 \cdot (1)))) \end{aligned}$$

The first four steps in this computation are recursive, with $n!$ being evaluated in terms of $(n-1)!$. The final step is not recursive, however. The following notation clearly distinguishes between the **recursive step** and the nonrecursive step (or **base case**) in the definition of $n!$:

$$n! = \begin{cases} 1 & \textit{if } n = 0 \textit{ (base case)} \\ n \cdot (n-1)! & \textit{if } n > 0 \textit{ (recursive step)} \end{cases}$$

The following program from the file *refactrl.cpp* uses recursion to compute the factorial of a number:

```
// Computes n! using a recursive factorial function.

#include <iostream.h>

long factorial ( int n );  // Function prototype

void main()
{
    int num = 4;    // Number whose factorial is to be computed.

    // Display the factorial of the number.
    cout << num << "! is " << factorial(num) << endl;
}

long factorial ( int n )
// Recursive factorial function.
{
    long result;
    if ( n == 0 )
        result = 1;                     // Base case
    else
        result = n * factorial(n-1);    // Recursive step
    return result;
}
```

The program issues the call `factorial(4)`. Because 4 is not equal to 0 (the condition for the base case), the `factorial()` function issues the recursive call `factorial(3)`. The recursive calls continue until the base case is reached—that is, until n equals 0.

```
factorial(4)
     ↓ RECURSIVE STEP
    4*factorial(3)
           ↓ RECURSIVE STEP
          3*factorial(2)
                 ↓ RECURSIVE STEP
                2*factorial(1)
                       ↓ RECURSIVE STEP
                      1*factorial(0)
                             ↓ BASE CASE
                             1
```

The calls to `factorial()` are evaluated in the reverse of the order in which they were made. The evaluation process continues until the value 24 is returned by the call `factorial(4)`.

```
factorial(4)
     ↑ Result = 24
    4*factorial(3)
           ↑ Result = 6
          3*factorial(2)
                 ↑ Result = 2
                2*factorial(1)
                       ↑ Result = 1
                      1*factorial(0)
                             ↑ Result = 1
                             1
```

WARM-UP EXERCISE

The greatest common divisor (GCD) of two positive integers *x* and *y* is the largest integer that evenly divides both *x* and *y*. A recursive definition elegantly expresses Euclid's algorithm for finding the GCD of two integers *x* and *y*:

$$GCD(x,y) = \begin{cases} x & \text{if } y = 0 \\ GCD(y, \text{ the remainder of } x \text{ divided by } y) & \text{if } y \neq 0 \end{cases}$$

Using this algorithm to compute *GCD*(30,12) generates the following sequence of calls and returns the value 6:

GCD(30,12)	GCD(30,12)
↓ RECURSIVE STEP	↑ RETURNS 6
GCD(12,6)	GCD(12,6)
↓ RECURSIVE STEP	↑ RETURNS 6
GCD(6,0)	GCD(6,0)
↓ BASE CASE	↑ RETURNS 6
6	6

In this exercise you use Euclid's algorithm to compute the GCD of a pair of integers.

`int gcd ( int x, int y )`

Input parameters
`x, y:` two integers
Returns
The greatest common divisor of x and y.

Complete the following program by filling in the missing C++ code. A shell for this program is given in the file *gcd.shl*.

```
// Computes the greatest common divisor (GCD) of two numbers using
// recursion.

#include <iostream.h>

int gcd ( int x, int y );

void main()
{
    int num1, num2;
    cout << "Enter two integers: ";
    cin >> num1 >> num2;

    // Display the GCD of num1 and num2.
    cout << ____________________________ << endl;
}
```

```
int gcd ( int x, int y )
{
    int result;
    if ( ____________ )
        result =________;            // Base case
    else
        result = ____________________;   // Recursive step
    return result;
}
```

PRESTIDIGITATION

A recursive function need not return a value. The following recursive definition describes an algorithm for outputting the digits in a positive integer in reverse order:

$$RightToLeft(n) = \begin{cases} \textit{Output } n & \textit{if } n < 10 \\ \textit{Output the remainder of } n \textit{ divided by } 10 & \textit{if } n \geq 10 \\ \textit{rightToLeft(the quotient of } n \textit{ divided by } 10) & \end{cases}$$

Note that in the second case (the recursive step) output is produced before the recursive call is made. Using this function to output the digits in the number 1384 generates the following sequence of calls and outputs the digits in reverse order (4831):

```
rightToLeft(1384)
    ↓ RECURSIVE STEP
  Outputs 4 rightToLeft(138)
                ↓ RECURSIVE STEP
              Outputs 8 rightToLeft(13)
                            ↓ RECURSIVE STEP
                          Outputs 3 rightToLeft(1)
                                        ↓ BASE CASE
                                      Outputs 1
```

Step 1: Create a function `rightToLeft()` that outputs the digits in an integer in reverse order. Base your function on the following specification:

`void rightToLeft ( int num )`

Input parameter

`num:` integer value

Outputs

Displays the digits in the number in reverse order, one per line.

Step 2: Add your `rightToLeft()` function to the test program in the file *testdig.cpp*.

Step 3: Complete the following test plan.

Test Plan for *rightToLeft()*			
Test case	*Sample data*	*Expected result*	*Checked*
Three-digit number	`123`	3 2 1	
Four-digit number			

A slight modification to your `rightToLeft()` function will produce the function specified below:

`void leftToRight ( int num )`
Input parameter
`num:` integer value
Outputs
Displays the digits in the number in order, one per line.

Step 4: Create the function `leftToRight()` specified above.

Step 5: Add your `leftToRight()` function to the test program in the file *testdig.cpp*.

Step 6: Complete the following test plan.

Test Plan for *leftToRight()*			
Test case	*Sample data*	*Expected result*	*Checked*
Three-digit number	`123`	1 2 3	
Four-digit number			

Laboratory 11: Bridge Exercise

TESTING AND DEBUGGING THE PRELAB APPLICATION EXERCISES

Date .... Section ....

Name ....

Ask your instructor whether you need to complete this exercise before your lab session or during lab.

PAINTING THE TOWN

Step 1: Execute the program in the file *testpnt.cpp*.

Step 2: Check each case in your *paintEstimate()* test plan, and verify the expected result. If you discover mistakes in your function, correct them and execute the test plan again.

BOXED IN

Step 1: Execute the program in the file *testbox.cpp*.

Step 2: Check each case in your *displayBox()* test plan, and verify the expected result. If you discover mistakes in your functions, correct them and execute the test plan again.

PRESTIDIGITATION

Step 1: Execute the program in the file *testdig.cpp*.

Step 2: Check each case in your *rightToLeft()* and *leftToRight()* test plans, and verify the expected result. If you discover mistakes in your functions, correct them and execute the test plans again.

Laboratory 11: In-lab Exercise 1

APPLYING PASS-BY-REFERENCE

Date .... Section ....

Name ....

STANDIN' ON SHAKY GROUND

The Richter scale expresses the intensity of an earthquake on a scale from 1 to 10. Unlike most scales that you are familiar with, the Richter scale is logarithmic, not linear. Thus an earthquake that produces a reading of 5.0 on the Richter scale is 10 times more powerful than an earthquake whose reading is 4.0.

You can compute the relative magnitude and the relative energy release of two earthquakes (*quake*1 and *quake*2) using the following formulas:

$$\textit{relative magnitude} = 10^{richter1-richter2}$$
$$\textit{relative energy} = 30^{richter1-richter2}$$

where *richter*1 and *richter*2 are the Richter scale readings for *quake*1 and *quake*2, respectively. Note that the *relative magnitude* is the magnitude of *quake*1 compared with *quake2*—that is, the ratio (magnitude *quake*1 / magnitude *quake*2)—and *relative energy* is the amount of energy released by *quake*1 compared with *quake*2.

Step 1: Create a function `compareQuakes()` that calculates the relative magnitude and relative energy of two earthquakes. Base your function on the following specification:

```
void compareQuakes ( double richter1, double richter2,
                     double &relMagnitude,
                     double &relEnergy                );
```

Input parameters

`richter1, richter2:` Richter scale readings for a pair of earthquakes

Output parameters

`relMagnitude:` magnitude of the first quake compared with the second

`relEnergy:` amount of energy released by the first quake compared with the second

Step 2: Add your `compareQuakes()` function to the test program in the file *testquak.cpp*.

Step 3: Test your function using the following test plan. If you discover mistakes in your function, correct them and execute the test plan again.

Test Plan for compareQuakes()			
Test case	*Sample data*	*Expected result*	*Checked*
Quake1: Southern Alaska, 1964 Quake2: San Francisco, 1906	`8.5` (est.) `8.3` (est.)	Quake1 was 1.58 times the magnitude of Quake2. Quake1 released 1.97 times the energy of Quake2.	
Quake1: Northwest Iran, 1990 Quake2: Central Mexico, 1985	`7.7` `8.1`	Quake1 was 0.4 times the magnitude of Quake2. Quake1 released 0.26 times the energy of Quake2.	
Quake1: Shaanxi Province, China, 1556 Quake2: Los Angeles, 1994	`8.6` (est.) `6.6`	Quake1 was 100 times the magnitude of Quake2. Quake1 released 900 times the energy of Quake2.	

Laboratory 11: In-lab Exercise 2

APPLYING RECURSION

Date .... Section ....

Name ....

C FOR YOURSELF

Many interesting graphic forms can be expressed easily using recursion. One such form is the C-curve, which is produced by recursively dividing a line segment into a set of successively shorter (and differently oriented) line segments.

The generation of a C-curve begins with a line segment. This line segment is replaced by a pair of line segments that are $1/\sqrt{2}$ the length of the original line and are oriented at a 90-degree angle to one another (note the "C" shape). Each of these line segments, in turn, is replaced by an additional pair of line segments. This process is repeated a finite number of times to produce a C-curve. Note that the C-curve becomes more visually complex and interesting the more levels of subdivision you perform.

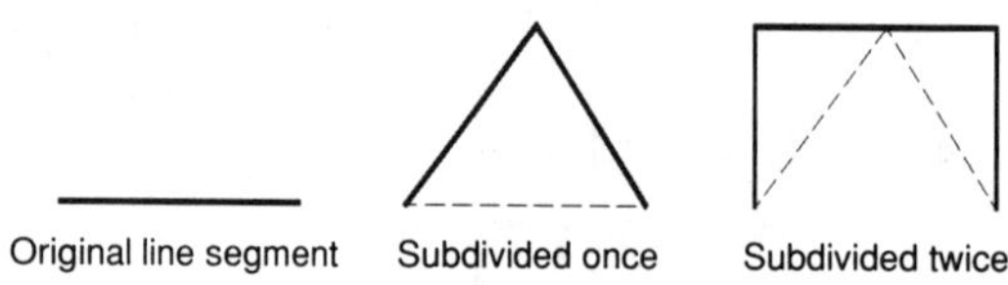

Expressing this process iteratively would be a daunting task. The recursive definition is quite succinct, however:

$$c\_curve(n, length, angle) \rightarrow \begin{cases} \textit{Draw a line segment with the specified} & \textit{if } n = 0 \\ \textit{length and orientation.} & \\ c\_curve(n-1, length/\sqrt{2}, angle + 45°) & \textit{if } n > 0 \\ c\_curve(n-1, length/\sqrt{2}, angle - 45°) & \end{cases}$$

Step 1: Create a function `c_curve()` that draws a C-curve. Base your function on the following specification:

```
void c_curve ( int n, double length, double angle )
```

Input parameters

`n:` number of recursive steps to perform

`length:` length of the line segment

`angle:` orientation of the line segment (measured from the *x*-axis in degrees)

Outputs

Displays the specified C-curve.

The base case of the C-curve definition ($n = 0$) requires drawing a line segment on the screen. Draw this line segment using a graphics function that draws a line from the current screen position to the point that lies Δx units away in the x-direction and Δy units away in the y-direction, where

$$\Delta x = length \cdot cos(angle)$$
$$\Delta y = length \cdot sin(angle)$$

In this way, the last point (pixel) in one line segment becomes the first point in the next line segment, and the line segments combine to form a C-curve.

Step 2: Add your `c_curve()` function to the test program in the file *testcurv.cpp*.

Step 3: Test your function using the following test plan. If you discover mistakes in your function, correct them and execute the test plan again. Note that the curve may be displayed upside down depending on the graphics coordinate system used.

Test Plan for *c_curve()*			
Test case	*Sample data*	*Expected result*	*Checked*
No recursive step	0	Draws the C-curve (line segment) shown on the left in the figure above	
One recursive step	1	Draws the C-curve in the middle	
Two recursive steps	2	Draws the C-curve on the right	

Laboratory 11: Postlab Exercise

POTENTIAL PITFALLS USING OVERLOADING AND RECURSION

Date .... Section ....

Name ....

PART A

The following function prototypes generate a compiler error:

```
float cube ( float x );
double cube ( float x );
```

Briefly explain the source of this error.

Why do you think overloading functions in this way is not permitted?

PART B

One mistake we sometimes make when we are first introduced to recursion is to use a while loop in place of an if-else selection structure, as in the following flawed recursive `factorial()` function.

```
long factorial ( int n )
// Flawed recursive factorial function.
{
    long result = 1;
    while ( n != 0 )
        result = n * factorial(n-1);
    return result;
}
```

What is wrong with this function?

Pointers and Strings

OVERVIEW

In previous laboratories you used variables containing data values of various types (`int`, `char`, and so forth). In this lab you work with pointer variables—that is, variables that contain the memory address of a data value rather than the data value itself. Pointer variables—or pointers, for short—are useful for efficiently manipulating array elements, processing strings, and dynamically allocating system memory (among other things).

In Prelab Exercise 1, you learn how to create pointer variables, dereference a pointer, and perform pointer arithmetic. In Prelab Exercise 2, you explore the use of pointers with functions and create a set of string processing functions. In Prelab Exercise 3, you use the operators `new` and `delete` to dynamically allocate memory.

LABORATORY 12: Cover Sheet

Date .... Section ....

Name ....

Place a checkmark in the *Assigned* column next to the exercises that your instructor has assigned to you. Have this sheet ready when your lab instructor checks your work. If your exercises are being checked outside the laboratory session, attach this sheet to the front of the packet of materials that you submit.

Exercise		*Assigned*	*Completed*
Prelab 1	What Is a Pointer?		
Prelab 2	Using Pointers with Functions		
Prelab 3	Dynamic Memory Allocation		
Bridge	Testing and Debugging the Prelab Application Exercises *Mirror Image* *Pulling Strings* *Tales from Decrypt*		
In-lab 1	Dynamic Array Allocation		
In-lab 2	Dynamic String Allocation		
Postlab	Analyzing Memory Allocation		
		Total	

Laboratory 12: Prelab Exercise 1

WHAT IS A POINTER?

Date .... Section ....

Name ....

BACKGROUND

The variables that you have worked with thus far contained data values. A pointer variable—or **pointer**—is different. Rather than containing a data value, a pointer contains the address in memory where a data value is stored.

You use the **indirection operator** `*` to declare a pointer variable. The declaration

```
int *iPtr;
```

creates a pointer named `iPtr` that can be used to store the address of an integer value. At this point (no pun intended), `iPtr` does not yet contain an address. One way you can assign an address to `iPtr` is by using the **address-of operator** `&`. The following code fragment, for example, assigns the address of the integer variable `num` to `iPtr`.

```
int *iPtr;      // iPtr is a pointer to an integer value
int num = 5;    // num contains the integer value 5
iPtr = &num;    // Make iPtr point to num
```

We say the `iPtr` "points to" `num`, as illustrated below:

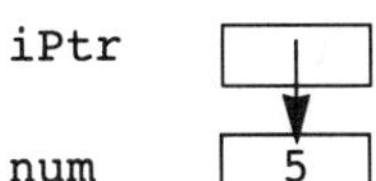

You use the indirection operator to access the value pointed to by a pointer. The statement

```
cout << *iPtr << endl;
```

uses the indirection operator to output the integer value (5) that is stored in the memory location (`num`) pointed to by `iPtr`. Accessing the value pointed to by a pointer is referred to as **dereferencing** a pointer, and the operator `*` is referred to as the **dereferencing operator**.

The contents of one pointer can be assigned to another pointer using the assignment operator. The statements

```
int *iPtr2;     // iPtr2 is a pointer to an integer value
iPtr2 = iPtr;   // Make iPtr2 point to what iPtr does (num)
```

for instance, create a second pointer, `iPtr2`, to the integer variable `num`.

In Laboratory 7 you saw that an array variable is actually a pointer to the first element in an array. The following code fragment begins by creating an array of characters called `heading`. It then assigns the address stored in the array variable `heading` to the character pointer `strPtr`.

```
char heading[11] = "A title",    // Sample string
     *strPtr;                    // Pointer to a char. in the string
strPtr = heading;
```

As a result, both `heading` and `strPtr` point to the first character in the array.

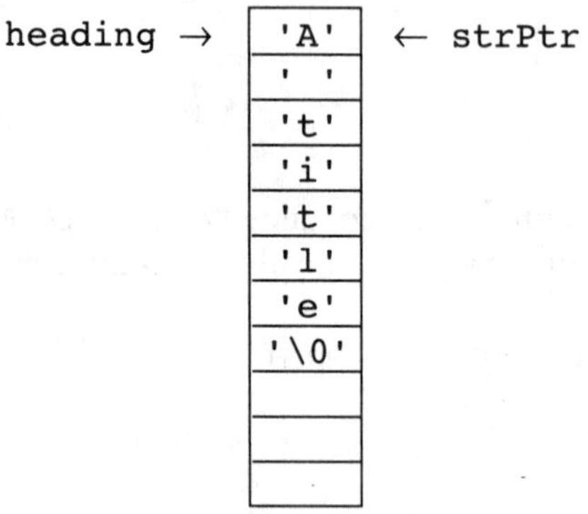

```
heading →  | 'A' |  ← strPtr
           | ' ' |
           | 't' |
           | 'i' |
           | 't' |
           | 'l' |
           | 'e' |
           | '\0'|
           |     |
           |     |
           |     |
```

Assignment is not the only operator you can use with pointers. You can also use C++'s predefined arithmetic operators to perform **pointer arithmetic**. The following program from the file *strprint.cpp* uses the increment operator to move a character pointer through a string character by character.

```
#include <iostream.h>

void main()
{
    char heading[11] = "A title",     // Sample string
         *strPtr;                     // Pointer to a character in
                                      // the string

    // Set strPtr to point to the first character in the string.
    strPtr = heading;

    // Display each character in the string. Stop when strPtr
    // points to the null character at the end of the string.
    while ( *strPtr != '\0' )
    {
       cout << *strPtr;    // Output the character pointed to by strPtr
       strPtr++;           // Advance to the next character
    }
    cout << endl;
}
```

Each time the statement

```
strPtr++;
```

is executed, the character pointer **strPtr** is advanced to the next character in the string. After three iterations through the loop, for example, **strPtr** points to the memory location containing the letter **'i'**.

```
heading → 'A'
          ' '
          't'
          'i'   ← strPtr
          't'
          'l'
          'e'
          '\0'
```

Individual characters in the string are accessed by applying the dereferencing operator to **strPtr**. The statement

```
cout << *strPtr;
```

uses the dereferencing operator to output the character pointed to by **strPtr**. The while loop condition

```
( *strPtr != '\0' )
```

uses this operator to check whether **strPtr** is pointing to the null character at the end of the string. When it does, the loop terminates, leaving **strPtr** pointing to the null character.

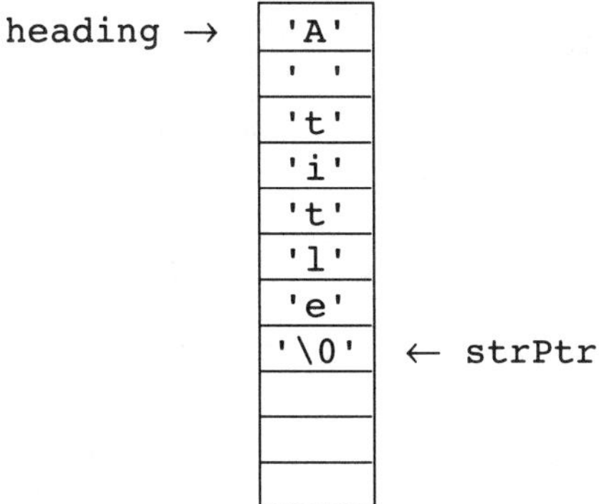

Adding the following code to the end of program *strprint.cpp* displays the string in reverse order.

```
// Pointer strPtr points to the null character at the end of the
// string. Move strPtr back one character so that it points to
// the last (non-null) character in the string.
strPtr--;

// Display the characters in the string in reverse order.
// Stop when strPtr moves past the beginning of the string.
while ( strPtr >= heading )
{
   cout << *strPtr;     // Output the character pointed to by strPtr
   strPtr--;            // Move back one character
}
cout << endl;
```

This code begins by using the decrement operator to move `strPtr` back one character, thereby making it point to the last character in the string. It then iterates through the characters in the string in reverse order until `strPtr` moves past the beginning of the string—that is, until `strPtr` is less than `heading`, as shown below:

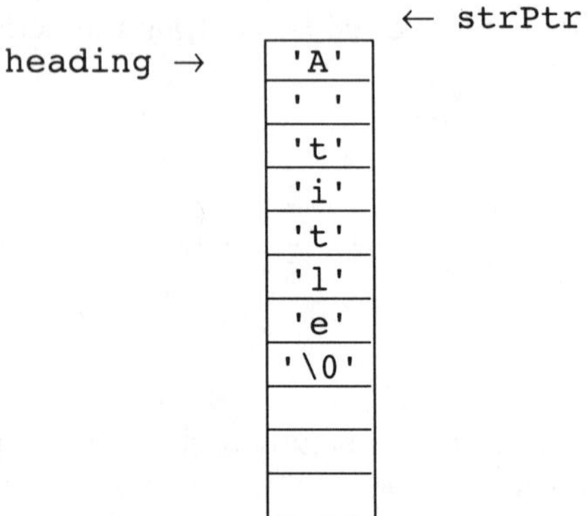

WARM-UP EXERCISE

Complete the following program by filling in the missing C++ code. A shell for this program is given in the file *strcount.shl*.

```
#include <iostream.h>

const int MAX_SIZE = 11;   // Maximum string length

void main()
{
    char inputString[MAX_SIZE],      // Input string
         ch,                         // Input character
         __________;                 // Pointer to a character in
                                     //   inputString
    int count = 0;                   // Number of times that ch occurs
                                     //   in inputString
```

```
    // Get a string from the user.
    cout << "Enter a string: ";
    cin >> inputString;

    // Get a character from the user.
    cout << "Enter a character: ";
    cin >> ch;

    // Count the number of times that character ch occurs in
    // inputString. Use a pointer to move through the string.
    for ( _______________; _______________; _______________ )
        if ( ____________ == ch )
           count++;

    // Output the count.
    cout << ch << " occurs " << count << " times in the string"
         << endl;
}
```

MIRROR IMAGE

A **palindrome** is a word, phrase, or sentence that reads the same backward or forward. Words that are palindromes include "a," "ewe," "toot," and "radar." Ignoring punctuation and spacing, the phrases "Able was I ere I saw Elba" and "A man, a plan, a canal, Panama" are both palindromes. The word "dodo" is not a palindrome because "dodo" ≠ "odod."

Step 1: Create a program that determines whether or not a word entered by the user is a palindrome.

Input: A word (maximum 10 letters)

Output: A message stating whether or not the word is a palindrome

Step 2: Save your program as *palindro.cpp*.

Step 3: Complete the following test plan.

Test Plan for *palindro*			
Test case	*Sample data*	*Expected result*	*Checked*
Five-letter palindrome			
Four-letter palindrome			
Word that is not a palindrome			

Laboratory 12: Prelab Exercise 2

USING POINTERS WITH FUNCTIONS

Date .... Section ....

Name ....

BACKGROUND

Passing a pointer to a function is similar to passing an array to a function. In both cases, you are passing the address where a data value (or values) is stored rather than the data value itself. The following function from the file *funcptr.cpp* takes two integer pointers and outputs the sum of the corresponding integer values. Note the use of the indirection operator in the parameter declarations and the use of the dereferencing operator in the computation of the sum.

```
void printSum ( int *numPtr1, int *numPtr2 )
{
    cout << *numPtr1 + *numPtr2 << endl;
}
```

Suppose that `val1` and `val2` are a pair of integer variables:

```
int val1 = 10,
    val2 = 20;
```

The call

```
printSum(&val1,&val2);
```

uses the address-of operator to generate the addresses of `val1` and `val2`. These addresses are passed to the function as the pointers `numPtr1` and `numPtr2`, and the sum of `val1` and `val2` is displayed.

When you are passing a pointer to a function, you are passing the address of a data value. As a result, any changes made using the pointer also change the data value. In other words, passing a pointer to a function passes the corresponding data value using pass-by-reference. The following function from the file *funcptr.cpp*

```
void swap (int *numPtr1, int *numPtr2)
{
    int temp;

    temp = *numPtr1;
    *numPtr1 = *numPtr2;
    *numPtr2 = temp;
}
```

uses this property to exchange the integer value pointed to by `numPtr1` with the value pointed to by `numPtr2`. The call

```
swap(&val1,&val2);
```

for instance, exchanges the values of `val1` and `val2`.

Using a pointer to pass a variable to a function using pass-by-reference was common programming practice in C. In C++, on the other hand, this parameter passing technique has been largely replaced by the use of reference parameters (see Laboratory 11), a language feature that does not exist in C. Using a pointer to pass a variable to a function using pass-by-reference is still commonly used when passing strings to a function, however. The following function from the file *funcptr.cpp* copies the contents of one string (`source`) to another (`dest`):

```
void copyString ( char *dest, char *source )
// Copies source string to dest string buffer. Note that strings
// source and dest are passed using pass-by-reference.
{
   while ( *source != '\0' )    // Stop when null reached in source
   {
      *dest = *source;     // Copy character
      source++;            // Advance to next character in source
      dest++;              // Advance to next character in dest
   }
   *dest = '\0';           // Add null character to dest
}
```

If `alpha` and `beta` are a pair of strings, that is,

```
char alpha[11] = "alpha",
     beta[11];
```

then the call

```
copyString(beta,alpha);
```

copies string `alpha` to `beta`.

Because pointer and array variables/parameters are essentially addresses, you can use the subscript operator—rather than the dereferencing operator—to access the individual characters in a string. The `copyString()` function, for example, can be rewritten using the subscript operator as follows:

```
void copyString ( char *dest, char *source )
// Copies source string to dest string buffer. Uses the subscript
// operator to access the characters in the strings.
{
   int index = 0;
   while ( source[index] != '\0' )     // Stop when null is reached
   {
      dest[index] = source[index];     // Copy character
      index++;                         // Advance to the next character
   }
   dest[index] = '\0';                 // Add null character to dest
}
```

In general, you can use either pointer or array notation to access the characters in a string. The notational style you choose depends on the nature of the function you are creating.

In addition to passing pointers to a function, a pointer also can be the result returned by a function. The following function from the file *funcptr.cpp* searches through a string for a specified character and returns a pointer to the first occurrence of the character. If the character does not occur in the string, then the function returns the **null pointer**—that is, the pointer value 0.

```
char *match ( char *str, char searchCh )
// Returns a pointer to the first character in string str that
// matches character searchCh. If there are no matches, then
// returns the null pointer.
{
    char *matchPtr = str;    // Pointer returned

    // Search for searchCh by advancing matchPtr through the string.
    while ( *matchPtr != searchCh  &&  *matchPtr != '\0' )
        matchPtr++;

    if ( *matchPtr == '\0' )
       matchPtr = 0;              // searchCh not found, return null

    return matchPtr;
}
```

The declaration

```
char *match ( .... )
```

specifies that the function's return value is a pointer to a character. When the `match()` function is invoked in the code fragment

```
char sample[11] = "Sample",
     *ptr;

ptr = match(sample,'p');
```

it returns a pointer to the character `'p'` and assigns this pointer to character pointer `ptr`.

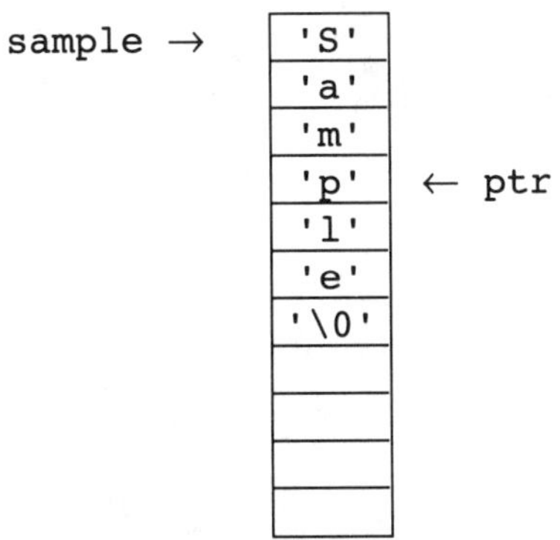

C++'s string library provides you with a set of useful string manipulation functions, several of which are described below. In order to use these functions, you must include the header file *string.h* in your program.

Function prototype	*Description*
`size_t strlen ( char *str )`	Returns the length of the string (excluding the null character)
`char *strcpy ( char *dest, const char *source )`	Copies string `source` to string `dest`. Returns a pointer to `dest`.
`char *strcat ( char *dest, const char *source )`	Concatenates string `source` to string `dest`. Returns a pointer to `dest`.
`int strcmp ( const char *s1, const char *s2, size_t n )`	Compares up to the first `n` characters of strings `s1` and `s2`. Returns 0 if the strings are the same, a value less than 0 if `s1` is less than `s2`, or a value greater than 0 if `s1` is greater than `s2`.
Note that `size_t` is defined by your C++ compiler to be an unsigned integer type such as `unsigned int` or `unsigned long`.	

WARM-UP EXERCISE

The following specification describes a function that reverses a string:

void strReverse (char *rdest, char *source)
Input parameter
source: the original string
Output parameter
rdest: the reversed string (the string buffer pointed to by **rdest** must be large enough to hold this string).

Complete the following program by filling in the missing C++ code for the function `strReverse()` specified above. A shell for this program is given in the file *revstr.shl*.

```
#include <iostream.h>
#include <string.h>                  //  For strlen()

const int STRING_SIZE = 11;          //  Max string length including the
                                     //  null terminator

void strReverse ( char *rdest, char *source );  // Function prototype

void main()
{
   char inputString[STRING_SIZE],         // String input by user
        reversedString[STRING_SIZE];      // Reversed string

   // Get the string from the user.
   cout << endl << "Enter a string: ";
   cin  >> inputString;

   // Reverse the string and display it.
   strReverse(reversedString,inputString);
   cout << "The string reversed is " << reversedString << endl;
}

void strReverse ( char *rdest, char *source )
{
                                          // Variable declarations



   // Insert code below that copies the characters from string
   // source into string rdest in reverse order.









   //  Add the null character to the end of string rdest.
   ________________ = '\0';
}
```

PULLING STRINGS

The following functions extract a portion of a string (a substring) and determine where two strings differ.

`void substring ( char *dest, char *source, int pos, int cnt )`
Input parameters
`source:` the original string
`pos:` the position at which to begin extracting characters
`cnt:` the number of characters to extract
Output parameter
`dest:` the extracted substring (the string buffer pointed to by `dest` must be large enough to hold this substring).

`char *differ ( char *s1, char *s2 )`
Input parameters
`s1, s2:` the strings to be compared
Returns
Returns a pointer to the first character in string `s1` that is different from the corresponding character in string `s2`. Returns the null pointer if the strings are identical or if `s1` is the same as the first *n* characters of `s2`, where *n* is the number of characters in `s1`.

Step 1: Create the functions `substring()` and `differ()` specified above.

Step 2: Add these functions to the test program in the file *teststr.cpp*.

Step 3: Complete the following test plan for the `substring()` function.

Test Plan for *substring()*			
Test case	*Sample data*	*Expected result*	*Checked*

Extract from middle of word	`stringer`
	`2`
	`4`
		Substring: `ring`	

Extract last half of word			
Extract entire word			

Step 4: Complete the following test plan for the `differ()` function.

Test Plan for *differ()*			
Test case	*Sample data*	*Expected result*	*Checked*
Strings differ at the third character	`stringer` `sting`	Pointer to character `'r'` in the first string	
Strings differ at the first character	`string` `ring`	Pointer to character `'s'` in the first string	
Strings are the same	`clone` `clone`	Null pointer	
First string is substring of the second	`string` `stringer`	Null pointer	

Laboratory 12: Prelab Exercise 3

DYNAMIC MEMORY ALLOCATION

Date .... Section ....

Name ....

BACKGROUND

In the programs you have created thus far, you have indicated at **compile-time** how much memory will be required to store the variables that are used in a given program. The following declarations, for instance, signal the compiler to reserve enough memory for a pair of integers, an array of 500 double-precision floating-point numbers, and a string containing 11 characters.

```
const int MAX_LENGTH = 11;
int num1;
double list[500];
char inputString[MAX_LENGTH];
```

This approach to memory allocation can be quite inefficient, especially when it comes to arrays and strings. Many times you do not know exactly how large an array needs to be until a program is actually running. Take the `list` array declared above as an example. It may be that this array is declared to be of length 500 simply because there are rare cases in which an array of this size is needed. Most of the time, however, a much smaller array will suffice. Rather than reserving as much memory as you think you might ever need—thereby wasting considerable amounts of memory most of the time—you would be better off specifying the size of the array at **run-time** and **dynamically allocating** the memory required by the array as the program executes.

In C++, you use the `new` **operator** to dynamically allocate memory for an array. When using the `new` operator, you specify the type of element stored in the array and the number of array elements (the size of the array). The `new` operator allocates the memory needed by the array and returns a pointer to the allocated memory. The statement

```
list = new double [listSize];
```

allocates an array containing `listSize` double-precision numbers and assigns `list` to point to the array, where `list` is of type `double*`. This statement is used in the following code fragment from the file *dynamic.cpp* to allocate an array whose length is specified at run-time by the user:

```
int listSize;     // Input list size
double *list;     // Pointer to dynamically allocated array

// Get the size of array needed.
cout << "Enter the array size: ";
cin >> listSize;

// Allocate an array of the specified size.
list = new double [listSize];
```

```
// Read in the array elements.
cout << "Enter the array elements: ";
for ( int j = 0 ; j < listSize ; j++ )
    cin >> list[j];
```

Whenever you allocate memory, you must ensure that it is deallocated once you no longer need it. You deallocate memory using the **`delete` operator**. The following statement releases the memory that you allocated for the `list` array in the code fragment above:

```
delete [] list;
```

Note the use of square brackets (`[ ]`) to signal that `list` points to an array rather than a single double-precision number.

WARM-UP EXERCISE

The following program dynamically allocates the memory needed to store a string. It asks the user how long the string will be and allocates just enough memory for a string of that length. Complete the program by filling in the missing C++ code. A shell for the program is given in the file *newstr.shl*.

```
#include <iostream.h>

void main()
{
    char __________;      // Pointer to a string
    int length;

    cout << endl
         << "Enter the number of characters in the string: ";
    cin >> length;

    // Allocate memory for the string. Remember to allow space
    // for the string delimiter.
    __________________________________________________;

    // Read in the string and echo it.
    cout << "Enter the string: ";
    cin >> ___________;
    cout << "Input string: " << ___________ << endl;

    // Deallocate the memory used to store the string.
    ______________________________;
}
```

TALES FROM DECRYPT

One of the first applications of computers was in the field of **cryptography**—that is, the science of creating and breaking codes. Encrypting a message entails transforming it into a form that is unintelligible to anyone who does not know the algorithm and secret key used in the encrypting process. The fact that the message is encrypted means that it can be sent over unsecured channels (radio, phone, computer network, mail, and so forth) because if it is intercepted it cannot be read. The intended recipient decrypts the message using the inverse of the algorithm used to encrypt it.

Most encryption algorithms require that both the sender and the recipient use the same key. This requirement, in turn, greatly complicates the encryption/decryption process because both parties must not only synchronize their use of keys—for example, all messages sent today use key A, those sent tomorrow use key B, and so forth—but also must communicate keys to one another at some point in time, thereby leading to the possibility of keys being lost or stolen.

A public-key encryption algorithm, on the other hand, uses a pair of keys—one that is known only to the recipient (the **secret key**) and one that is known to everyone (the **public key**). When you wish to send a message to a particular person, you begin by looking up that person's public key. You then encrypt the message using this key and transmit the message. The recipient uses his or her secret key to decrypt the message.

$$\text{Message} \xrightarrow[\text{the public key}]{\text{encrypted using}} \text{encrypted message} \xrightarrow[\text{the secret key}]{\text{decrypted using}} \text{original message}$$

The RSA public-key cryptosystem ("RSA" are the last initials of the developers: Rivest, Shamir, and Adleman) uses a pair of very large integers (*B, P*) as the public key and another pair of very large integers (*B, S*) as the secret key. Note that by "very large" we mean hundreds of digits. You begin the encryption process by breaking a message up into numbers that are smaller than the bounding value *B*. You then encrypt each piece of the message *M* using the formula

$$E = M^P \bmod B$$

and transmit the encrypted message *E*. The recipient uses the formula

$$M = E^S \bmod B$$

to decrypt the encrypted message, yielding the original message *M*.

Let's look at an example using the following unrealistically small values for *B, P,* and *S*.

$$B = 143, P = 47, \text{and } S = 23$$

We send the message `"HI"` as two integers 48 and 49 (the ASCII codes for `'H'` and `'I'`, respectively). These are encrypted as follows:

$$\texttt{'H'} : 48^{47} \bmod 143 \rightarrow 41$$

$$\texttt{'I'} : 49^{47} \bmod 143 \rightarrow 83$$

When the recipient receives the encrypted message (41,83) she or he decrypts it, as follows:

$$41^{23} \bmod 143 \rightarrow 48 : \texttt{'H'}$$

$$83^{23} \bmod 143 \rightarrow 49 : \texttt{'I'}$$

Note that practical applications of this algorithm use much larger values for *B, P,* and *S*—values hundreds of digits long. As a result, the message is ordinarily sent in large pieces rather than as individual characters.

Step 1: Create a program that decrypts a message that has been encrypted character by character using the RSA public-key cryptosystem with $B = 143$, $P = 47$, and $S = 23$. Your program should begin by reading in the number of integer values in the encrypted message. It should then read in the encrypted message and store it in a message buffer—in this case, an array of integers. Once the message has been read in, your program should decrypt it using the `decryptRSA()` function given in the file *decrypt.shl* and store the resulting decrypted message in another message buffer—this one an array of characters. Finally, your program should output the decrypted message.

Base your program on the program shell given in the file *decrypt.shl*. Note that both message buffers should be dynamically allocated based on the length of the message.

Input: The number of integer values (encrypted characters) in the encrypted message
The encrypted message

Output: The decrypted message

Step 2: Save your program in the file *decrypt.cpp*.

Step 3: Complete the following test plan.

Test Plan for *decrypt*			
Test case	*Sample data*	*Expected result*	*Checked*
Message length: 9	`78 118 44 95 76 72 67 54 132`	Nice job!	
Message length: 17	`83 52 79 95 76 38 67 129 76 37 76 58 95 44 82 95 129`	I've got a secret	

Laboratory 12: Bridge Exercise

TESTING AND DEBUGGING THE PRELAB APPLICATION EXERCISES

Date .... Section ....

Name ....

Check with your instructor whether you need to complete this exercise before your lab session or during lab.

MIRROR IMAGE

Step 1: Execute your program in the file *palindro.cpp*.

Step 2: Check each case in your *palindro* test plan, and verify the expected result. If you discover mistakes in your program, correct them and execute the test plan again.

PULLING STRINGS

Step 1: Execute the program in the file *teststr.cpp*.

Step 2: Check each case in your *substring()* test plan, and verify the expected result. If you discover mistakes in your function, correct them and execute the test plan again.

Step 3: Check each case in your *differ()* test plan, and verify the expected result. If you discover mistakes in your function, correct them and execute the test plan again.

TALES FROM DECRYPT

Step 1: Execute your program in the file *decrypt.cpp*.

Step 2: Check each case in your *decrypt* test plan, and verify the expected result. If you discover mistakes in your program, correct them and execute the test plan again.

Laboratory 12: In-lab Exercise 1

DYNAMIC ARRAY ALLOCATION

Date .... Section ....

Name ....

I'VE GOT A SECRET

In Prelab Application Exercise 3, you used the RSA public-key cryptosystem algorithm to decrypt a message. In this exercise, you use the same cryptosystem to encrypt a message.

Step 1: Create a program that encrypts a message character by character using the RSA public-key cryptosystem with $B = 143$, $P = 47$, and $S = 23$. Your program should begin by reading in the number of characters in the message. It should then read in the encrypted message and store it in a message buffer—in this case, an array of characters. Once the message has been read in, your program should encrypt it using the `encryptRSA()` function given in the file *encrypt.shl* and store the resulting encrypted message in another message buffer—this one an array of integers. Finally, your program should output the encrypted message.

Base your program on the program shell given in the file *encrypt.shl*. Note that both message buffers should be dynamically allocated based on the length of the message. Note also that if you want to be able to handle messages containing whitespace you will need to use the input stream member functions `get()` and/or `getline()` to read in the message (see Laboratory 10).

Input: The number of characters in the message
The message

Output: The encrypted message

Step 2: Save your program in the file *encrypt.cpp*.

Step 3: Test your program using the following test plan. If you discover mistakes in your function, correct them and execute the test plan again.

Test Plan for *encrypt*			
Test case	*Sample data*	*Expected result*	*Checked*
Message length: 16	Congratulations!	111 67 11 38 82 37 129 39 114 37 129 118 67 11 58 132	
Message length: 9	Nice job!	78 118 44 95 76 72 67 54 132	
Message length: 17	I've got a secret		

Laboratory 12: In-lab Exercise 2

DYNAMIC STRING ALLOCATION

Date .... Section ....

Name ....

BUFFERIN'

The `strcpy()` function in the string library copies a string into an existing string buffer. The function defined below differs from `strcpy()` in that it dynamically allocates a new buffer in which to place the copy. The allocated buffer is just large enough to hold the string.

`char *strNewCopy ( char *source )`
Input parameter
`source:` the original string
Returns
A pointer to a dynamically allocated string buffer containing a copy of the string

Step 1: Create the function `strNewCopy()` specified above.

Step 2: Add your `strNewCopy()` function to the test program *testcopy.cpp*.

Step 3: Test your function using the following test plan. If you discover mistakes in your function, correct them and execute the test plan again.

Test Plan for *strNewCopy()*			
Test case	*Sample data*	*Expected result*	*Checked*
A four-character string	`four`		
A five-character string			

Laboratory 12: Postlab Exercise

ANALYZING MEMORY ALLOCATION

Date .... Section ....

Name ....

PART A

Solving each of the following problems requires the use of an array. Can the length of the array be specified at compile-time or should the array be dynamically allocated at run-time? Explain the reasoning behind your answers.

1. Read through a document character by character. As you read through the document, keep track of the number of times that each letter appears. When you are done, output the number of times each letter appeared in the document.

2. For an arbitrary class, read in the name and exam score for each student in the class and output the student records in descending order based on exam score.

PART B

What is wrong with the following program and how would you correct this problem?

```
#include <iostream.h>

void main()
{
    char *strPtr;

    // Read in a string.
    cin >> strPtr;

    // Output the input string.
    cout << strPtr;
}
```

Classes II

OVERVIEW

In Laboratory 9 you studied the basics of how classes are created and applied. You implemented a `TextWindow` class and used this class as part of a program that displayed information on the screen. In this lab you explore some of the more advanced features of C++ classes.

In Prelab Exercise 1, you overload the constructor for the `TextWindow` class by adding a default constructor along with a complementary function that allows the user to set the position of a text window's boundaries. In Prelab Exercise 2, you examine how to overload C++ operators to support `Point` and `TextWindow` objects. Prelab Exercise 3 explores inheritance—a mechanism that allows you to build a new class from an existing class. In this exercise you derive a `PushButton` class from your `TextWindow` class.

LABORATORY 13: Cover Sheet

Date .... Section ....

Name ....

Place a checkmark in the *Assigned* column next to the exercises that your instructor has assigned to you. Have this sheet ready when your lab instructor checks your work. If your exercises are being checked outside the laboratory session, attach this sheet to the front of the packet of materials that you submit.

Exercise		*Assigned*	*Completed*
Prelab 1	Default Constructors		
Prelab 2	Operator Overloading		
Prelab 3	Inheritance		
Bridge	Testing and Debugging the Prelab Application Exercises *No Argument Here* *Smooth Operator* *Derived Pleasure*		
In-lab 1	Client Functions		
In-lab 2	Arrays of Objects		
Postlab	Class Composition		
		Total	

Laboratory 13: Prelab Exercise 1

DEFAULT CONSTRUCTORS

Date .... Section ....

Name ....

BACKGROUND

In Laboratory 9 you specified the values of an object's data members when the object was created—that is, when the object was declared and its constructor invoked. The `Point` class constructor, for instance, sets a point's *x*- and *y*-coordinates to the values specified by the constructor's `xCoord` and `yCoord` parameters:

```
Point::Point ( int xCoord, int yCoord )
// Constructor.
{
    x = xCoord;
    y = yCoord;
}
```

In some cases, however, you want a constructor that simply initializes an object's data members to some predetermined (default) values. Such a constructor has no arguments and is referred to as a **default constructor**. Default constructors ensure that an object's data members are in a known state. For example, a default `Point` constructor might initialize a point's *x*- and *y*-coordinates to (0, 0):

```
Point::Point ()
// Default constructor. Sets point to (0,0).
{
    x = 0;
    y = 0;
}
```

The declaration

```
Point pt1;
```

invokes the `Point` default constructor to create a point `pt1` and initialize it to (0, 0).

Classes that have default constructors usually also have **set functions** that assign values to an object's data members. The following set function specifies a point's *x*- and *y*-coordinates:

```
void Point::setXY ( int newX, int newY )
// Sets a point's x- and y-coordinates to the specified values.
{
    x = newX;
    y = newY;
}
```

You might use this function to set point `pt1` to (2, 4), as follows:

```
pt1.setXY(2,4);
```

Note that the `setXY()` function can be applied repeatedly to assign a series of values to a point. The following code fragment, for instance, uses point `pt1` to create a crude display of the curve $y = x^2$:

```
for ( j = 0 ; j < 10 ; j++ )
{
    pt1.setXY(j,j**j);
    pt1.display();
}
```

WARM-UP EXERCISE

The following program uses the `Point` default constructor and `setXY()` function to display a series of user-input points. Complete the program by filling in the missing C++ code. A shell for this program is given in the file *testdef.shl*. Prototypes for the default constructor and the `setXY()` function are given in the `Point` class declaration in the header file *point2.h,* and implementations of these functions are given in the file *point2.cpp*.

```
#include <iostream.h>
#include "point2.h"

void main()
{
    int inputX,      // Input coordinates
        inputY;

    // Declare a point inputPt using the default constructor.
    ________________________________;

    // Read in a series of point coordinates and display them.
    // Stop when the point (0,0) is input.
    cout << endl << "Input the x- and y-coordinates for a point: ";
    cin >> inputX >> inputY;
    while ( inputX != 0  || inputY != 0 )
    {
        // Set the coordinates of inputPt to inputX and inputY.
        ________________________________________;

        // Display inputPt's data members.
        inputPt.showDataMembers(); cout << endl;

        // Get the next point.
        cout << " Input the x- and y-coordinates for a point: ";
        cin >> inputX >> inputY;
    }
}
```

NO ARGUMENT HERE

In this exercise you create a default constructor and a set function for your `TextWindow` class. Because you can use your `replaceText()` function to set (or reset) a text window's text string, your `TextWindow` set function only needs to set the positions of the window's edges.

Step 1: Copy your implementation of the `TextWindow` class (in the file *twindow.cpp*) to the file *twindow2.cpp*.

Step 2: Change the `#include` directive in the file *twindow2.cpp* so that the header file *twindow2.h* is included in place of the header file you used in Laboratory 9.

Step 3: Implement the `TextWindow` default constructor specified below. A prototype for this function is given in the `TextWindow` class declaration in the header file *twindow2.h*.

`TextWindow ()`

Requirements
None
Results
Default constructor. Creates an empty text window (null text string) that occupies the entire screen.

Step 4: Add this function to your `TextWindow` class implementation in the file *twindow2.cpp*.

Step 5: Implement the following `TextWindow` member function. A prototype for this function is given in the `TextWindow` class declaration in the header file *twindow2.h*.

```
void setEdges ( int leftEdge, int topEdge, int rightEdge,
                int bottomEdge                           )
```

Requirements
None
Results
Sets the positions of a text window's edges to `leftEdge`, `topEdge`, `rightEdge`, and `bottomEdge`.

Step 6: Add this function to your `TextWindow` class implementation in the file *twindow2.cpp*.

Step 7: Complete the following test plan for the default constructor and `setEdges()` function.

Test Plan for *Test 1*			
Test case	*Sample data*	*Expected result*	*Checked*
Create a default text window			
Set the window's edges to create a smaller window			

Laboratory 13: Prelab Exercise 2

OPERATOR OVERLOADING

Date .... Section ....

Name ....

BACKGROUND

You declare an object as a function parameter in the same way you declare any other function parameter—you specify the type of object (its class) and the name of the parameter. For example, the following function determines whether two points are the same distance from the origin.

```
int equidistant ( Point pt1, Point pt2 )
// Returns 1 if pt1 and pt2 are the same distance from (0,0).
// Otherwise, returns 0.
{
    return ( pt1.distance() == pt2.distance() );
}
```

Note that the `equidistant()` function is *not* a member function of the `Point` class. It does, however, use `Point` objects and public member functions. Functions such as this one are referred to as **client functions** of the `Point` class. You work more with client functions in In-lab Exercise 2.

Just as an object can be passed to a client function, it also can be passed to a member function. The following `Point` member function determines whether two points are the same—that is, whether they have the same *x*- and *y*-coordinates.

```
int Point::sameAs ( Point rightPt )
// Returns 1 if rightPt has the same coordinates as a point.
// Otherwise, returns 0.
{
    return ( x == rightPt.x  &&  y == rightPt.y );
}
```

The following code fragment uses this function to compare two points.

```
if ( alpha.sameAs(beta) )
   cout << "Points are the same" << endl;
else
   cout << "Points are different" << endl;
```

When `sameAs()` is invoked, `rightPt` contains a copy of `beta`. The references in the `return` statement are then resolved as follows:

```
return ( x == rightPt.x  &&  y == rightPt.y );
        /         /          /          \
    alpha.x      /        alpha.y        \
                /                         \
  rightPt.x (copy of beta.x)      rightPt.y (copy of beta.y)
```

Both `alpha` and `rightPt` are `Point` objects (as is `beta`, for that matter). The `sameAs()` function is a member function of the `Point` class. As a result, it can legally access any `Point` object's data members—including `alpha`'s and `rightPt`'s.

In the preceding example, `beta` is passed to the `sameAs()` function using pass-by-value. Passing an object using pass-by-value requires copying the object, a task that can become quite costly in terms of time and storage if the object is large—a text window, for instance. It is common programming practice in C++ to eliminate the copying of arguments by using **pass-by-`const`-reference** whenever possible, as in the following function:

```
int Point::sameAs ( const Point &rightPt )
// Returns 1 if rightPt has same coordinates as a point.
// Otherwise, returns 0.
{
    return ( x == rightPt.x  &&  y == rightPt.y );
}
```

With pass-by-`const`-reference, the address of an argument—rather than a copy of the argument—is passed to a function. The `const` designation means that the function cannot alter the value of the argument (or its data members). Note that in changing the function to use pass-by-`const`-reference, we did not change the body of the function, only its parameter list.

You may have noticed that the syntax for comparing two points using `sameAs()` is somewhat awkward and nondescriptive. We are much more accustomed to expressing equality in the following way:

```
if ( alpha == beta )
   cout << "Points are the same" << endl;
else
   cout << "Points are different" << endl;
```

Fortunately, C++ allows you to create operators that share the name of one of its predefined operators, but that manipulate your objects rather than one of C++'s predefined types—an ability referred to as **operator overloading**. The following function, for example, overloads the equality operator (==) to handle `Point` objects.

```
int Point::operator == ( const Point &rightPt )
// Returns 1 if rightPt has same coordinates as a point.
// Otherwise, returns 0.
{
    return ( x == rightPt.x  &&  y == rightPt.y );
}
```

You specify the operator to be overloaded using the keyword `operator` followed by the operator symbol (==). You also provide a return type—in this case `int`—just as you would for any other function. The compiler automatically uses this version of the == operator whenever it is asked to determine whether two `Point` objects are equal.

WARM-UP EXERCISE

The following `Point` member function overloads the assignment operator (`=`) to handle `Point` objects.

`void operator = ( const Point &rightPt )`

Requirements
None
Results
Assigns (copies) the contents of `rightPt` to a point.

Step 1: Complete the following function by filling in the missing C++ code. A shell for this function is given in the file *point2.cpp.*

```
void Point::operator = ( const Point &rightPt )
// Assigns (copies) rightPt to a point.
{
    _______________________;    // Assign rightPt's x-coordinate
    _______________________;    // Assign rightPt's y-coordinate
}
```

Step 2: Complete the following program by filling in the missing C++ code. A shell for this program is given in the file *testops.shl.*

```
#include <iostream.h>
#include "point2.h"
void main()
{
    // Declare a point named point1 and initialize its coordinates to
    // (20,10).
    ________________________________;

    // Declare a point named point2 using the default constructor.
    ________________________________;

    // Test if the two points are equal.
    if ( _____________________________ )
       cout << "The points have the same coordinates" << endl;
    else
       cout << "The points have different coordinates" << endl;

    // Assign the coordinates of point1 to point2.
    _________________________________;
```

```
    // Test if the two points are equal.
    cout << "After assignment -- ";
    if ( ______________________________ )
       cout << "the points have the same coordinates" << endl;
    else
       cout << "the points have different coordinates" << endl;
}
```

SMOOTH OPERATOR

In this exercise you overload the equality operator (==) to test if two `TextWindow` objects have the same dimensions and text string.

Step 1: Implement the overloaded equality operator specified below for your `TextWindow` class. A prototype for this function is given in the `TextWindow` class declaration in the header file *twindow2.h*.

`int operator == ( const TextWindow &rightWindow )`

Requirements
None
Results
Returns 1 if `rightWindow` has the same dimensions (width and height) and text string as a text window. Otherwise, returns 0.

Step 2: Add this function to your `TextWindow` class implementation in the file *twindow2.cpp*.

Step 3: Complete the following test plan for the equality (`==`) operator.

Test Plan for *Test 2*			
Test case	*Sample data*	*Expected result*	*Checked*
Same edges, same text		Window 1 == Window 2 : 1 Window 2 == Window 1 : 1	
Same dimensions (different edges), same text		Window 1 == Window 2 : 1 Window 2 == Window 1 : 1	
Different dimensions, same text		Window 1 == Window 2 : 0 Window 2 == Window 1 : 0	
Same edges, different text		Window 1 == Window 2 : 0 Window 2 == Window 1 : 0	
Different dimensions, different text		Window 1 == Window 2 : 0 Window 2 == Window 1 : 0	

Laboratory 13: Prelab Exercise 3

INHERITANCE

Date .... Section ....

Name ....

BACKGROUND

A key feature of any object-oriented language is the ability to derive a new class from an existing one through **inheritance**. The **derived class** inherits the member functions and data members of the existing **base class** and can have its own member functions and data members as well. In this exercise you use C++'s inheritance mechanism to create derived classes from your `Point` and `TextWindow` classes.

Suppose you want to create a smiley face that you can move around the screen. You could create an entirely new class with member functions for constructing, moving, positioning, and drawing a smiley face. A better option is for you to derive a `Smiley` class from your `Point` class, thereby inheriting the existing `move()` and `setXY()` member functions (among others) from `Point`. This inheritance relationship is expressed in the following class declaration from the file *smiley.h*.

```
class Smiley : public Point
{
  public:

    Smiley ( int xCoord, int yCoord, char symbol );     // Constructor
    void setMouth ( char symbol );                      // Set mouth
    void draw ();                                       // Draw smiley

  private:

    // Data member
    char mouth;      // Mouth symbol
};
```

The `Smiley` class supplies its own constructor as well as its own member functions `setMouth()` and `draw()`. It also has a private data member `mouth` that specifies the character to be used when drawing the smiley's mouth.

The declaration

```
class Smiley : public Point
```

indicates that the `Smiley` class is derived from the `Point` class. The keyword `public` specifies that this is a **public inheritance**—that is, the `Smiley` class inherits the `Point` class's public member functions but *not* its private data members. You want the member functions in

`Smiley`—the `draw()`function in particular—to be able to refer to the private data members in `Point`, so you must change the data members in the `Point` class declaration from private to protected as follows:

```
class Point
{
  public:           // Member functions
    ...

  protected:        // Data members

      int x;        // x-coordinate
      int y;        // y-coordinate
};
```

In a public inheritance, `Point`'s private data members can only be accessed by `Point`'s member functions, but `Point`'s **protected** data members can be accessed by the member functions in any class that is derived from `Point`—in this case, the `Smiley` class.

A `Smiley` object can call any of `Point`'s public member functions, as well as any of its own (`Smiley`) public member functions. For example, the following code fragment repositions the object `face` at (15,8) and changes its mouth to `'('` (sad).

```
Smiley face(5,7,')');   // Classic smiley face at (5,7)
...
face.setXY(15,8);       // Reposition at (15,8) -- Point member function
face.setMouth('(');     // Make the face sad -- Smiley member function
```

Before you can use the `Smiley` class, you need to implement its constructor, `setMouth()`, and `draw()` member functions. The `Smiley` class's constructor

```
Smiley::Smiley ( int xCoord, int yCoord, char symbol )
// Constructor.
  : Point(xCoord,yCoord),     // Initialize coordinates
    mouth(symbol)             // Initialize mouth symbol
{}
```

uses an **initialization list** to call the `Point` class's constructor and to initialize the `mouth` data member. Note that a colon appears at the start of the initialization list, the items in the list are separated by commas, and there is *no* semicolon at the end of the list. You implement the `setMouth` and `draw()` member functions in the Warm-up Exercise.

WARM-UP EXERCISE

Step 1: Complete the `Smiley setMouth()` and `draw()` member functions by filling in the missing C++ code. A shell for these functions is given in the file *smiley.cpp*.

```
void Smiley::setMouth ( char symbol )
// Sets the mouth to the specified symbol.
{



}


void Smiley::draw ()
// Draws a smiley face at point (x,y) on the screen.
{






}
```

Step 2: Complete the following program by filling in the missing C++ code. A shell for this program is given in the file *testsmil.shl*.

```
#include <iostream.h>
#include "smiley.h"

void main ()
{
    // Declare a smiley named face whose coordinates are the center
    // of the screen and whose mouth is happy (')').
    __________________________;

    // Draw the face.
    face.draw();

    // Move the face to the lower left-hand corner of the screen.
    ________________________________;

    // Change to a grim ('|') face.
    _________________________________;

    // Redraw the face.
    face.draw();
}
```

DERIVED PLEASURE

User interfaces provide various controls for selecting features, specifying options, and so forth. A **push button** control has two states: on and off. You shift between these states by pressing the button using a mouse click or keystroke combination. The following class declaration from the file *button.h* derives a `PushButton` class from your `TextWindow` class.

```
class PushButton : public TextWindow
{
  public:

    PushButton ( int left, int top, char label[] );    // Constructor
    void push();                                       // Press button

  private:

    // Data member
    int status;    // Button status (0=unselected, 1=selected)
};
```

The constructor and `push()` function are specified below.

`PushButton ( int left, int top, char label[] )`

Requirements
None
Results
Constructor. Creates an unselected push button with the specified label. The size of the window is determined by the length of the label. Assumes that the label does *not* contain any vertical bars (`'|'`) and that it begins with three blanks (to leave room for the asterisk that is used to indicate when a button is selected).

`void push()`

Requirements
None
Results
Pushes a button. If it was unselected, it becomes selected, and if it was selected, it becomes unselected.

The following code fragment creates a sample button, displays it, pushes the button, and displays it again.

```
PushButton sample(10,10,"   Sample button");
sample.display();
sample.push();
sample.display();
```

The resulting buttons are shown below.

Before `push()`: After `push()`:

```
Sample button
```

```
* Sample button
```

Note that the `push()` function changes both the button's `status` data member and the button window's `text` data member.

Step 1: Change the data members in your `TextWindow` class declaration in the file *twindow2.h* from private to protected.

Step 2: Implement the constructor and `push()` function specified above, and save them in the file *button.cpp*. Prototypes for these functions are given in the `PushButton` class declaration in the file *button.h*.

Step 3: Fill in the missing coordinates in the test program in the file *testpush.shl*, save the resulting program as *testpush.cpp*, and complete the following test plan.

Test Plan for *PushButton*

Test case	*Sample data*	*Expected result*	*Checked*
Display a push button labeled "Hit Return" in the upper left-hand portion of the screen			
Push the button on, move it down and to the right, and redisplay the button			
Push the button off, move it down and to the right, and redisplay the button			

Laboratory 13: Bridge Exercise

TESTING AND DEBUGGING THE PRELAB APPLICATION EXERCISES

Date .... Section ....

Name ....

Check with your instructor whether you need to complete this exercise before your lab session or during lab.

Step 1: Compile your implementation of the `TextWindow` class in the file *twindow2.cpp*.

Step 2: Compile the test program in the file *testwin2.cpp*.

Step 3: Link the object files produced by steps 1 and 2.

NO ARGUMENT HERE

Step 1: Compile the implementation of the `TextWindow` class (in the file *twindow2.cpp*) and the test program in the file *testwin6.cpp*. Link the resulting object files to produce an executable file.

Step 2: Check each case in the test plan for *Test 1* (default constructor and `set'Edges'`() function), and verify the expected result. If you discover mistakes in your implementation, correct them and execute the test plan again.

SMOOTH OPERATOR

Step 1: Compile the implementation of the `TextWindow` class (in the file *twindow2.cpp*) and the test program in the file *testwin7.cpp*. Link the resulting object files to produce an executable file.

Step 2: Check each case in the test plan for *Test 2* (equality (==) operator), and verify the expected result. If you discover mistakes in your implementation, correct them and execute the test plan again.

DERIVED PLEASURE

Step 1: Compile your implementation of the `TextWindow` class in the file *twindow2.cpp*.

Step 2: Compile your implementation of the `PushButton` class in the file *button.cpp*.

Step 3: Compile the test program in the file *testpush.cpp*.

Step 4: Link the object files produced by steps 1, 2, and 3.

Step 5: Execute the file produced by step 4.

Step 6: Check each case in your *PushButton* test plan, and verify the expected result. If you discover mistakes in your implementation, correct them and execute the test plan again.

Laboratory 13: In-lab Exercise 1

CLIENT FUNCTIONS

Date .... Section ....

Name ....

GOOD AS GOLD

In this exercise you create a pair of **client functions**—functions that are not members of a class but that act on objects in the class using the class's public member functions. The following client function tests if two points are the same distance from the origin.

```
int equidistant ( Point pt1, Point pt2 )
// Returns 1 if pt1 and pt2 are the same distance from (0,0).
// Otherwise, returns 0.
{
    return ( pt1.distance() == pt2.distance() );
}
```

This function is passed two `Point` objects, `pt1` and `pt2`. Because `equidistant()` is not a member of the `Point` class, it does *not* have direct access to `Point`'s private data members. It does have access to `Point`'s public member functions, however, and it uses one of these, `distance()`, to compute the distance from each point to the origin.

The functions specified below are client functions of the `TextWindow` class. Both functions have `TextWindow` objects as function parameters. The `makeGolden()` function also returns a `TextWindow` object.

`int wider ( TextWindow w1, TextWindow w2 )`

Inputs
`w1, w2:` a pair of text windows
Returns
Returns 1 if `w1` is wider than `w2`. Otherwise, returns 0.

`TextWindow makeGolden ( TextWindow w )`

Inputs
`w:` a text window
Returns
A text window whose width and upper left-hand corner are the same as window `w`'s but whose lower right-hand corner is moved so that the ratio of the window's width to its height is approximately the golden ratio defined below.

$$\textit{Golden ratio} = \frac{1 + \sqrt{5}}{2}$$

Note that the golden ratio occurs frequently in classical architecture and art. It was viewed as producing forms that have a certain harmony and visual appeal.

Step 1: Implement these functions, and save them in the file *twclient.cpp*. Prototypes for these functions are given in the file *twclient.h*.

Step 2: Test your `wider()` function using the test program in the file *testwcf1.cpp* and the following test plan. If you discover mistakes in your function, correct them and execute the test plan again.

Test Plan for *wider()*			
Test case	*Sample data*	*Expected result*	*Checked*
Window1 is 60 x 15 Window2 is 45 x 15		Window1 is wider than Window2 : 1 Window2 is wider than Window2 : 0	
Window2 is 10 x 20 Window1 is 30 x 10		Window1 is wider than Window2 : 0 Window2 is wider than Window2 : 1	
Window1 and Window2 are both 10 x 20		Window1 is wider than Window2 : 0 Window2 is wider than Window2 : 0	

Step 3: Test your `makeGolden()` function using *testwcf2.cpp* and the following test plan. If you discover mistakes in your function, correct them and execute the test plan again.

Test Plan for *makeGolden()*			
Test case	*Sample data*	*Expected result*	*Checked*
Increase window height to produce golden ratio		Input window : width = 26 height = 10 Window returned: width = 26 height = 16	
Decrease window height to produce golden ratio		Input window : width = 34 height = 24 Window returned: width = 34 height = 21	

Laboratory 13: In-lab Exercise 2

ARRAYS OF OBJECTS

Date .... Section ....

Name ....

INDEX CARDS

You can create an array of objects in much the same way that you create arrays of integers, characters, and so forth. The following program from the file *ptarray.cpp* reads in an array of points. These points might represent the vertices of a polygon or an outline of a curve, for instance.

```
#include <iostream.h>
#include "point2.h"

void main ()
{
    const int MAX_NUM_POINTS = 5;     // Maximum number of points
    Point pt[MAX_NUM_POINTS];         // Array of points
    int inputX,                       // Input x- and y-coordinates
        inputY,
        j;                            // Loop counter

    // Read in the coordinate pairs.
    for ( j = 0 ; j < MAX_NUM_POINTS ; j++ )
    {
        cout << "Enter the coordinates for pt[" << j << "]: ";
        cin >> inputX >> inputY;
        pt[j].setXY(inputX,inputY);
    }
}
```

You declare an array of objects by giving the type of object followed by the name of the array and its size. The declaration

```
Point pt[MAX_NUM_POINTS];         // Array of points
```

creates an array of points named `pt` containing `MAX_NUM_POINTS` points. Note that the default `Point` class constructor is automatically called for each point in the array.

The program asks the user to input a series of *x*- and *y*-coordinates. After each coordinate pair is entered, the program uses the `setXY()` function to store it in an array element. If the user enters the following coordinate pairs, for example,

```
 6 3
 8 4
10 5
12 6
14 7
```

the array of points would contain the following data:

pt[0]	(6,3)
pt[1]	(8,4)
pt[2]	(10,5)
pt[3]	(12,6)
pt[4]	(14,7)

In this exercise you use your `TextWindow` class to create and display an array containing five note cards.

Step 1: Create a program that reads the text for five note cards from the keyboard and displays the note cards on the screen (where on the screen is up to you). All the note cards are the same size (the size is up to you).

Input: The text for five note cards

Output: The note cards are displayed on the screen

A sample output screen is shown below.

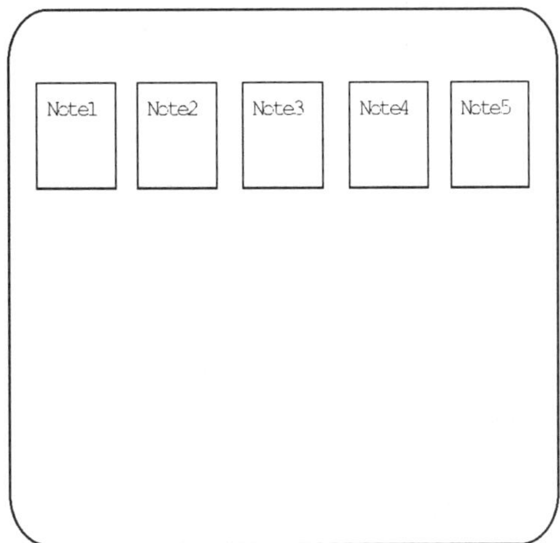

Step 2: Save your program as *notecard.cpp*.

Step 3: Test your program using the following test plan. If you discover mistakes in your program, correct them and execute the test plan again.

Test Plan for *notecard*			
Test case	*Sample data*	*Expected result*	*Checked*

Five note cards	`Note1`
	`Note2`
	`Note3`
	`Note4`
	`Note5`		

Your five note cards			

Laboratory 13: Postlab Exercise

CLASS COMPOSITION

Date .... Section ....

Name ....

A triangle can be described by three points. Specify the member functions and data members for a new `Triangle` class based on your `Point` class (note that inheritance is not needed).

PART A

Give function specifications for the member functions that form the public interface to your `Triangle` class. Be sure to include a constructor.

PART B

List the private data members that you would include in your `Triangle` class. Briefly describe the information stored in each data member.

Team Software Development Project

OVERVIEW

The programs you developed in previous labs solved very specific problems. These programs tended to be relatively short, and you were able to create them by yourself directly from the problem descriptions. As problems become more complex, however, team programming efforts and formal program designs become necessary parts of the program development process.

In this lab you work with other students as part of a software development team that designs and implements a programming project using object-oriented design and programming techniques. The intent of the lab is for you to see how a complex problem can be solved by decomposing it into a set of interrelated objects and to give you a feel for the dynamics of a team programming environment.

The program development process is done over the space of two weeks. During the first week, you work with your teammates to create a program design. In the second week, you implement your design to form a working program.

LABORATORY 14 – WEEK 1: Cover Sheet

Date .... Section ....

Name ....

List the members assigned to your software development team and the class (or classes) that each team member designs in the Bridge Exercise. Attach one copy of this sheet to the front of your team's design.

Team member / Section	*Classes designed*	*Completed*

LABORATORY 14 — WEEK 3: CONCLUSION

Laboratory 14 — Week 1: Prelab Exercise

OBJECT-ORIENTED DESIGN

Date .... Section ....

Name ....

BACKGROUND

Given a complex problem, how do you begin to develop a program to solve the problem? Unfortunately, there is no simple answer to this question. How you look at the problem, what form you imagine the solution will take, and what programming language and techniques you intend to use—all of these shape not only the solution, but also the process of finding a solution.

In this lab you use a program development style called **object-oriented programming** in which you analyze a problem in terms of the objects in the problem. An **object** is something with a well-defined set of **attributes** and **behaviors**. A statue, a car, a fish, a movie, a party, and a trip—all of these are examples of objects from the real world. We humans are expert at thinking about the world around us in terms of objects. **Object-oriented design** (OOD) and **object-oriented programming** (OOP) attempt to apply this ability to the design and creation of programs.

Rather than discussing object-oriented design in the abstract, let's try to find the objects in the following problem:

> Part of a children's math education program is a calculator that displays a sad face whenever the number displayed by the calculator is negative and a happy face whenever the number displayed is positive. The calculator responds to the following commands (where *num* is a floating-point number): +*num*, –*num*, **num*, /*num*, and C (clear). In addition, the child can use the Q (quit) command to end the program.

One object is obvious: the calculator. What attributes and behaviors are associated with the calculator? This depends on who is doing the associating—different people will produce different results. One possible set of attributes and behaviors is shown below.

Object: Calculator
Attributes: Number displayed (the accumulator)
Behaviors: Performs arithmetic operations
Displays number

What other objects are there? The problem refers to a display that shows a happy or sad face depending on the number stored in the calculator's accumulator. This face display is another object.

Object: Face
Attributes: Happy or sad
Behaviors: Changes face to happy
Changes face to sad
Displays face

Could we have combined the Calculator and Face objects into one object? Yes. The process of finding and using objects is not one with rigid rules. We chose a definition of calculator that fits a broad range of calculators, not just the one discussed in this problem. Other choices may be equally valid, however.

Finding the final object requires a little effort. Something must be coordinating the actions of the Calculator and Face objects based on the commands input by the child. This object is commonly called the interface.

Object: Interface
Attributes: Calculator
Face
Command
Behaviors: Coordinates the calculator and face displays
Reads a command
Executes the command

Now that we have identified a set of objects, we need to develop a C++ class for each object. As a general rule, an object's attributes become data members of the corresponding class, and its behaviors become member functions. Keep in mind, however, that in program design there are no inflexible rules, only guidelines.

Let's start with the Face object. This object has an attribute that indicates whether the face is a happy face or a sad one. It has behaviors that display the face and change it to happy or to sad. We represent the Face object using a C++ class called `Face` in which the happy/sad attribute is represented by an integer data member `state`, and the behaviors are represented by the member functions `display()`, `makeHappy()`, and `makeSad()`. The declaration for the `Face` class and the specifications for its member functions are shown below. Note that we have included a constructor that initializes a face to happy when it is declared (constructed).

```
class Face
{
  public:

    Face ();                // Constructor
    void makeHappy ();      // Set face to happy
    void makeSad ();        // Set face to sad
    void display ();        // Display face

  private:

    // Data member
    int state;              // Face state (1=happy, 0=sad)
};
```

`Face ()`
Requirements
None
Results
Constructor. Creates a face and initializes it to happy.

`void makeHappy ()`
Requirements
None
Results
Changes a face to happy.

`void makeSad ()`
Requirements
None
Results
Changes a face to sad.

`void display ()`
Requirements
None
Results
Displays a face.

Continuing with the Calculator object, we represent this object's accumulator attribute by a double-precision floating-point data member `accum` and its behaviors by the member functions `add()`, `subtract()`, `multiply()`, `divide()`, `clear()`, and `display()`. We complete the set of member functions by adding a constructor and an access function `value()`. The constructor initializes the accumulator to zero, and the `value()` function communicates the accumulator's value to other classes.

```
class Calculator
{
  public:

    Calculator ();                      // Construct calculator
    void add ( double num );            // Add to accumulator
    void subtract ( double num );       // Subtract from accumulator
    void multiply ( double num );       // Multiply accumulator
    void divide ( double num );         // Divide accumulator
    void clear ();                      // Clear accumulator
    double value ();                    // Return accumulator
    void display ();                    // Display calculator

  private:

    // Data member
    double accum;     // Accumulator
};
```

`Calculator ()`
Requirements
None
Results
Constructor. Creates a calculator and initializes its accumulator to zero.

`void add ( double num )`
Requirements
None
Results
Adds num to the accumulator.

`void subtract ( double num )`
Requirements
None
Results
Subtracts num from the accumulator.

`void multiply ( double num )`
Requirements
None
Results
Multiplies the accumulator by num.

`void divide ( double num )`
Requirements
The value of num is not zero.
Results
Divides the accumulator by num.

`void clear ()`
Requirements
None
Results
Clears the accumulator (sets it to zero).

`double value ()`
Requirements
None
Results
Returns the value stored in the accumulator.

`void display ()`
Requirements
None
Results
Displays a calculator.

We create the `Interface` class in much the same way we did the `Calculator` and `Face` classes. In this case, we represent the calculator, face, and command attributes by three data members: `calc`, `smiley`, and `userCmd`.

```
class Interface
{
  ...
    // Data members
    Calculator calc;     // Calculator object
    Face smiley;         // Face object
    Command userCmd;     // User command
};
```

The first two data members are instances of classes that we have defined rather than instances of one of C++'s predefined data types. One of the virtues of C++ is that this difference has little or no impact on how we declare (or later use) the `Interface` class. We simply treat the classes we develop as though they are built into C++. The `userCmd` data member stores the last command the user entered along with the command's argument (if any) in the following structure:

```
struct Command
{
    char cmd;       // Command name (letter)
    double arg;     // Command argument
};
```

We represent the Interface object's behaviors by the member functions `generateDisplay()`, `getCommand()`, and `executeCommand()`. To these we add a constructor that initializes the data members and a `done()` function that indicates when the child has entered the Q (quit) command. The declaration for the `Interface` class and the specifications for its member functions are given below.

```
class Interface
{
  public:

    Interface ();                  // Constructor
    void generateDisplay ();       // Generate interface display
    void getCommand ();            // Get user command
    void executeCommand ();        // Process user command
    int done ();                   // Exit interface

  private:

    // Data members
    Calculator calc;     // Calculator object
    Face smiley;         // Face object
    Command userCmd;     // User command
};
```

`Interface ()`
Requirements
None
Results
Constructor. Creates an interface and initializes its data members.

`void generateDisplay ()`
Requirements
None
Results
Generates an interface display consisting of a calculator and a happy/sad face.

`void getCommand ()`
Requirements
None
Results
Prompts the user for a command, reads in a command from the keyboard, and stores it in `userCmd`.

`void executeCommand ()`
Requirements
None
Results
Executes the user's last command (in `userCmd`).

`int done ()`
Requirements
None
Results
Returns 1 if the user has entered the Q (quit) command. Otherwise, returns 0.

We now have a set of well-defined classes for the children's calculator problem. Taken together, these object descriptions, class declarations, and function specifications provide a **design** for one solution to this problem. In Week 2's Background section we will explore how to implement this solution. Given a good design, developing an implementation is an easy task. Given a bad design, it is a difficult, if not impossible, job. That is why the design development process is so important—in many ways it is the art that defines computer science. Creativity and insight in the design phase lead to programs that are easy to implement and maintain. More important, they result in programs that are enjoyable to use. Mistakes made in the design phase, on the other hand, are costly to fix and often yield a poor product.

WARM-UP EXERCISE

A stoplight is a familiar object on our roadways. Define the attributes and behaviors for a stoplight below.

Object: Stoplight
Attributes:

Behaviors:

DESCRIPTION OF THE PROGRAMMING PROJECT

Computer monitors often become note boards covered with scraps of paper listing important facts, meetings, and so forth. Rather than coating your monitor with these notes, it would be more convenient—and much neater—to store (and retrieve) the information using a simple user-friendly notes program.

In this lab you and your teammates complete a programming project in which you design and implement a calendar notes program that features a calendar display to which you affix a set of notes. Each note is one line long (40 characters maximum), and you can associate up to 10 notes with a given calendar.

The program begins by asking the user for the name of a file containing a set of notes. It then displays the calendar for the current month, retrieves the notes associated with this calendar from the notes file, and displays these notes on a note board beside the calendar. A sample display is shown below.

```
 December          1995

 S   M   T   W   T   F   S
                     1   2
 3   4   5   6   7   8   9
10  11  12  13  14  15  16
17  18  19  20  21  22  23
24  25  26  27  28  29  30
31
```

```
----- Commands -----
P          Prev month
N          Next month
<          Prev year
>          Next year
G fname    Get file
A note     Add note
Q          Quit
```

```
Poetry paper due on the 8th.

CS final 12/13 at 9AM

Check on preregistration

Get school T-shirt for kid brother

12/15 Going home!!!!!!
```

```
Enter command:
```

The user controls the program using the keyboard commands listed below. After executing a command, the program clears the screen, displays a calendar, retrieves the notes associated with this calendar from the notes file, and displays a note board containing these notes. By recreating the entire screen, the program avoids changing only parts of the screen, a task that is difficult in some environments.

Command	*Action*	*Description*
P	Preceding month	Changes the calendar to the preceding month.
N	Next month	Changes the calendar to the next month.
<	Preceding year	Changes the calendar to the preceding year.
>	Next year	Changes the calendar to the next year.
G *filename*	Get notes file	Changes the notes file to the specified file.
A *note*	Add note	Adds the specified note to the current notes file. Associates the note with the calendar currently being displayed.
Q	Quit	Quits the program.

Although the commands are shown using uppercase letters, the user can input the commands using lowercase letters as well. If the user enters a command other than those shown above, the program outputs the message "Invalid command." The program also displays a meaningful error message if the user attempts to associate more than 10 notes with a given calendar. Error messages are displayed for 2 seconds and then erased.

The notes in a notes file are stored one per line using the following format:

month year note

where *month* and *year* specify the calendar that the note is associated with and *note* is a maximum of 40 characters. The file *notes.dat* contains a sample notes file.

In order to produce a calendar for a given month, you need to know on which day of the week the first day of the month occurs. You can compute the day of the week corresponding to a date *month*/*day*/*year* using the following formula:

$$DayOfWeek = (1 + nYears + nLeapYears + nDaysToMonth + day) \% 7$$

where *nYears* is the number of years since 1901, *nLeapYears* is the number of leap years since 1901, and *nDaysToMonth* is the number of days from the start of the year to the start of *month*.

This formula yields a value between 0 (Sunday) and 6 (Saturday) and is accurate for any date from January 1, 1901 to December 31, 2099. You can compute the value *nDaysToMonth* dynamically using a loop. Alternatively, you can use an array to store the number of days before each month in a non-leap year and add a correction for leap years when needed. Note that in this project you are concerned with dates of the form *month*/1/*year*—that is, the first day of a given month.

UNIDENTIFIED OBJECTS

Step 1: Identify the objects in the programming project. Be sure to look for objects that are not described explicitly in the problem statement but which are implicitly part of the problem. Often these kinds of objects provide the means (information or actions) by which other objects interrelate. The role played by the Interface object in the children's calculator problem is typical of these kinds of objects.

Step 2: Define each object's attributes and behaviors.

Laboratory 14 — Week 1: Bridge Exercise

DESIGNING CLASSES

Date .... Section ....

Name ....

Check with your instructor whether you need to complete this exercise before your lab session or during lab. Your instructor will either assign you to a software development team or provide you with guidelines for forming a team.

Step 1: In the Prelab Exercise each member of your team created a set of objects for the programming project—including object attributes and behaviors. Review the sets of objects produced by you and your teammates. Focus your discussion on the similarities and differences in how each of you saw the problem and created objects. Did you produce different numbers of objects? If so, why? How do the objects differ in terms of their attributes and their behaviors? Are these differences serious or merely cosmetic?

Remember that there are no rigid rules for the design process. Different people see problems in different ways. These diverse perspectives, in turn, shed considerably more light on a problem than does a single view.

Step 2: Combine your team's efforts and create *one* set of objects for the programming project. Produce a document listing the objects, their attributes, and their behaviors. Use the object description format shown in the Background section of the Prelab Exercise.

Step 3: Assign each object to a team member. Each team member will design and implement a C++ class for each of her or his assigned objects, so try to balance the projected workload equitably among team members.

Step 4: Design a C++ class for each of your assigned objects. For each class, provide the following information:

- A brief description of the class focusing on what the class does and how it is used.
- A C++ class declaration, including data members and member functions.
- A detailed function specification for each member function. Use the function specification format shown in the Background section of the Prelab Exercise.
- A list of the other classes that use this class (its **clients**).
- A list of the other classes that this class uses (its **collaborators**).

Laboratory 14 — Week 1: In-lab Exercise

DESIGN SYNTHESIS

Date .... Section ....

Name ....

CLASS REVIEW

Step 1: Review the classes you produced in the Bridge Exercise with your teammates. Pay particular attention to how each class relates to its clients and its collaborators.

Relationship of a class to its clients:

- Do its member functions perform the tasks required by its clients?
- Is the class missing any member functions, or does it have extra (unused) member functions?
- Is it clear what each member function does and how it is to be used?
- Does the class maintain the information needed by its clients?
- Do the clients have a way of accessing this information?

Relationship of a class to its collaborators:

- Does each collaborator perform the tasks needed by the class?
- How is each collaborator used?
- How does the class access the information maintained by each collaborator?

Step 2: Combine your team's efforts to produce a team design for the programming project. Base the organization of your design on the following outline.

Week 1 Cover Sheet

Object descriptions (one for each object)

Class descriptions (one for each class)

LABORATORY 14 - WEEK 2: Cover Sheet

Date .... Section ....

Name ....

List the members assigned to your software development team and the class (or classes) each team member implements in the Prelab Exercise. Attach one copy of this sheet to the front of your team's implementation document.

Team member / Section	*Classes implemented*	*Completed*

Laboratory 14 — Week 2: Prelab Exercise

OBJECT-ORIENTED PROGRAMMING

Date .... Section ....

Name ....

BACKGROUND

In the Background section for Week 1 you saw how object-oriented design (OOD) methods can be used to design a children's calculator program. The resulting design consisted of three interrelated classes: `Calculator`, `Face`, and `Interface`. Our task now is to implement the member functions in these classes and the calculator program's `main()` function.

We begin by saving the class declarations for the `Calculator`, `Face`, and `Interface` classes in the header files *calc.h*, *face.h*, and *interf.h*, respectively (the declaration for the `Command` structure also is placed in *interf.h*). Later on we will store our implementations of these classes in the files *calc.cpp*, *face.cpp*, and *interf.cpp*. Note that *face.h* and *face.cpp* combine to form the `Face` class, *calc.h* and *calc.cpp* combine to form the `Calculator` class, and *interf.h* and *interf.cpp* combine to form the `Interface` class.

Let's start the implementation process with the `Calculator` class. This class's member functions are quite simple—no surprises here. The `display()` function forms the calculator using standard characters. This approach allows for generality of use—every environment supports text output—at the price of visual pizzazz.

```
// Implementation of the Calculator class

#include <iostream.h>
#include <iomanip.h>
#include "calc.h"

//--------------------------------------------------------------------

Calculator::Calculator ()
// Constructor. Creates a calculator and initializes its accumulator
// to zero.
{
    accum = 0;
}

//--------------------------------------------------------------------

void Calculator::add ( double num )
// Adds num to the accumulator.
{
    accum += num;
}
```

```
//----------------------------------------------------------------

void Calculator::subtract ( double num )
// Subtracts num from the accumulator.
{
    accum -= num;
}

//----------------------------------------------------------------

void Calculator::multiply ( double num )
// Multiplies the accumulator by num.
{
    accum *= num;
}

//----------------------------------------------------------------

void Calculator::divide ( double num )
// Divides the accumulator by num.
{
    accum /= num;
}

//----------------------------------------------------------------

void Calculator::clear ()
// Clears the accumulator (sets it to zero).
{
    accum = 0;
}

//----------------------------------------------------------------

double Calculator::value ()
// Returns the value stored in the accumulator.
{
    return accum;
}

//----------------------------------------------------------------

void Calculator::display ()
// Displays a calculator.
{
    cout << "----------------" << endl;
    cout.setf(ios::fixed);
    cout << "|" << setw(12) << accum << "  |" << endl;
    cout << "|              |" << endl;
    cout << "|  1  2  3  +  |" << endl;
    cout << "|  4  5  6  -  |" << endl;
    cout << "|  7  8  9  *  |" << endl;
    cout << "|     0  C  /  |" << endl;
    cout << "----------------" << endl;
}
```

Implementing the **Face** class is an equally straightforward task. In this case, the **display()** function outputs the smiley face you saw in Laboratory 1 using both its happy and sad incarnations.

```
// Implementation of the Face class

#include <iostream.h>
#include "face.h"

//--------------------------------------------------------------------

Face::Face()
// Constructor. Creates a face and initializes it to happy.
{
    makeHappy();
}

//--------------------------------------------------------------------

void Face::makeHappy ()
// Changes a face to happy.
{
    state = 1;
}

//--------------------------------------------------------------------

void Face::makeSad ()
// Changes a face to sad.
{
    state = 0;
}

//--------------------------------------------------------------------

void Face::display ()
// Displays a face.
{
    if ( state == 1 )
       cout << ":-)";
    else
       cout << ":-(";
}
```

Implementing the **Interface** class is a little trickier. Recall that this class has three data members **calc**, **smiley**, and **userCmd**. Data members **calc** and **smiley** are instances of the **Calculator** and **Face** classes, and **userCmd** is a **Command** structure. The **Interface** class constructor initializes the command name (**userCmd.cmd**) to the null command.

```
Interface::Interface ()
// Constructor. Creates an interface and initializes its data members.
{
    userCmd.cmd = '\0';
}
```

The `generateDisplay()` member function uses the `display()` member functions in the `Face` and `Calculator` classes to display the smiley face followed by the calculator. Note that additional formatting is done to center the smiley face above the calculator.

```
void Interface::generateDisplay ()
// Generates an interface display consisting of a happy/sad face and
// a calculator.
{
    cout << endl << "          ";
    smiley.display();
    cout << endl;
    calc.display();
}
```

User commands are read from the keyboard by the `getCommand()` member function. If a command has a numeric argument, this argument is read in as well. The input command and argument (if any) are stored in `userCmd`.

```
void Interface::getCommand ()
// Prompts the user for a command, reads in a command from the
// keyboard, and stores it in userCmd.
{
    cout << "Enter command: ";
    cin >> userCmd.cmd;
    if ( userCmd.cmd == '+'  ||  userCmd.cmd == '-'  ||
         userCmd.cmd == '*'  ||  userCmd.cmd == '/'     )
       cin >> userCmd.arg;
}
```

The `executeCommand()` member function processes the user's last command. This function must rely on the member functions of the `Face` and `Calculator` classes to modify the `smiley` and `calc` objects.

```
void Interface::executeCommand ()
// Executes the user's last command (in userCmd).
{
    switch ( userCmd.cmd )
    {
      case '+' :  calc.add(userCmd.arg);       break;
      case '-' :  calc.subtract(userCmd.arg);  break;
      case '*' :  calc.multiply(userCmd.arg);  break;
      case '/' :  if ( userCmd.arg != 0 )
                     calc.divide(userCmd.arg);
                  else
                     cout << "Cannot divide by 0" << endl;
                  break;
      case 'C' :
      case 'c' :  calc.clear();  break;
      case 'Q' :
      case 'q' :  break;
      default  :  cout << "Invalid command" << endl;
    }
    if ( calc.value() < 0 )    // Update the face
       smiley.makeSad();
    else
       smiley.makeHappy();
}
```

Finally, clients of the `Interface` class test whether the user has input the Q (quit) command using the `done()` member function.

```
int Interface::done ()
// Returns 1 if the user has entered the Q (quit) command. Otherwise,
// returns 0.
{
    return ( userCmd.cmd == 'Q'  ||  userCmd.cmd == 'q' );
}
```

Having completed our implementation of the `Face`, `Calculator`, and `Interface` classes, all we need to do is create a `main()` function that moves the interface through repetitions of the following three-step cycle: generate display, get command, and process command.

```
// Main program for the children's calculator program

#include "interf.h"

void main ()
{
    Interface cmdInterface;    // Interface object

    while ( !cmdInterface.done() )
    {
        cmdInterface.generateDisplay();
        cmdInterface.getCommand();
        cmdInterface.executeCommand();
    }
}
```

At this point we have completed development of the children's calculator program. The question that now arises is, "How do we test and debug our program?" Rather than throwing everything together and testing the entire program, we use the same strategy to test that we used to develop the program. First, we test each class. Once we've worked out the bugs in the individual classes, we combine them, and test the complete program.

We begin by developing a simple test program for each class. The test program should provide us with the ability to check each member function using various input values. A simple interactive test program for the `Calculator` class is given below:

```
// Test program for the Calculator class

#include <iostream.h>
#include "calc.h"

void main ()
{
    Calculator calc;     // Calculator object
    char oper;           // Input operator
    double num;          // Input number

    // Test the arithmetic functions and the value() function.
    cout << endl << "Start of testing" << endl;
    do
    {
        calc.display();
        cout << endl << "Enter operator ( Q0 to end ) : ";
        cin >> oper >> num;
```

```
        switch ( oper )
        {
          case '+' :  calc.add(num);       break;
          case '-' :  calc.subtract(num);  break;
          case '*' :  calc.multiply(num);  break;
          case '/' :  calc.divide(num);    break;
        }
        cout << "Calculator value : " << calc.value() << endl;
    }
    while ( oper != 'Q'  &&  oper != 'q' );

    // Test the clear() function.
    calc.clear();
    cout << endl << "Calculator cleared" << endl;
    calc.display();
}
```

Testing the `Interface` class is somewhat more difficult because this class contains data members that are instances of other classes. Two strategies can be applied here; one is to complete testing and debugging of the `Face` and `Calculator` classes before starting to test the `Interface` class. Unfortunately, this approach forces the developer of the `Interface` class to wait for the developers of the other classes to finish their work before she or he is even able to compile the `Interface` class implementation.

A better strategy is to develop test stubs for the `Face` and `Calculator` classes and to use these stubs in the initial testing of the `Interface` class. A **test stub** for a class is an "implementation" of the class's member functions in which each function simply outputs the fact that it is called and returns a value (if the function is not void). Part of the test stub for the `Calculator` class is shown below:

```
// Test stub for the Calculator class

#include <iostream.h>
#include "calc.h"

//--------------------------------------------------------------------

Calculator::Calculator ()
// Constructor. Creates a calculator and initializes the accumulator
// to zero.
{
    cout << "Calculator constructor called" << endl;
}

//--------------------------------------------------------------------

double Calculator::value ()
// Returns the value stored in the accumulator.
{
    cout << "Calculator::value() called" << endl;
    return 0;
}
//--------------------------------------------------------------------

void Calculator::add ( double num )
// Adds num to the accumulator.
{
    cout << "Calculator::add() called" << endl;
}
...
```

You can easily create a test stub from a class declaration. Note that you do not need to know how you will actually implement the member functions in order to create the test stub. As simple as these test stub member functions are, they provide enough information for developers whose routines use your class to begin testing their efforts.

WARM-UP EXERCISE

The following files contain the class declarations, implementations, test stubs, and test programs for the classes developed above.

Class	*Header file*	*Test stub*	*Implementation*	*Test program*
`Face`	*face.h*	*facestub.cpp*	*face.cpp*	*testface.cpp*
`Calculator`	*calc.h*	*calcstub.cpp*	*calc.cpp*	*testcalc.cpp*
`Interface`	*interf.h*		*interf.cpp*	*testintf.cpp*

Step 1: Informally test (no test plan required) the implementation of the `Face` class in the file *face.cpp* using the test program in the file *testface.cpp.*

Step 2: Informally test the implementation of the `Calculator` class in the file *calc.cpp* using the test program in the file *testcalc.cpp.*

Step 3: Informally test the implementation of the `Interface` class in the file *interf.cpp* using the test stubs in the files *facestub.cpp* and *calcstub.cpp* and the test program in the file *testintf.cpp.*

Step 4: Having completed testing of these classes, informally test the children's calculator program using the class implementations in the files *face.cpp*, *calc.cpp*, and *interf.cpp* and the `main()` function in the file *kidcalc.cpp.*

BUILDING CODE

During the first week of this Lab you and your teammates developed a design for the programming project. This week, each team member implements and tests the classes that she or he designed last week. You then combine your efforts to produce a complete program.

Step 1: Save the class declaration for each of your classes in an appropriately named header file. Give copies of these header files to all your teammates.

Step 2: Create a test stub for each of your classes. Give copies of these test stubs to all your teammates.

Step 3: Implement the member functions for each of your classes. The team member whose class manages the user interface also should implement the program's `main()` function. Be sure to document your code.

Step 4: Create a test program and a test plan for each of your classes. A blank test plan form is given on the next page.

Should you make any changes to a class—by adding a data member or a member function, for instance—be certain to inform your teammates in a timely manner.

Test Plan for the Class			
Test case	*Sample data*	*Expected result*	*Checked*

Laboratory 14 — Week 2: Bridge Exercise

TESTING AND DEBUGGING YOUR CLASSES

Date .... Section ....

Name ....

Check with your instructor whether you need to complete this exercise before your lab session or during lab.

Test each of the classes you implemented in the Prelab Exercise. Use your test program for the class to check each case in the class's test plan, and verify the expected result. If you discover mistakes in an implementation, correct them and execute the test plan again.

Laboratory 14 — Week 2: In-lab Exercise

IMPLEMENTATION SYNTHESIS

Date .... Section ....

Name ....

PUTTING IT ALL TOGETHER

Step 1: Combine your tested class implementations with your teammates' efforts to produce a complete program.

Step 2: Work with your teammates to develop a test plan for the programming project. A blank test plan form is given on the next page.

Step 3: Execute your team's program. Check each case in your test plan, and verify the expected result. If you discover mistakes in your team's program, correct them and execute the test plan again.

Step 4: Create an implementation document that contains the source code and test plans for your team's program. Base the organization of your document on the following outline:

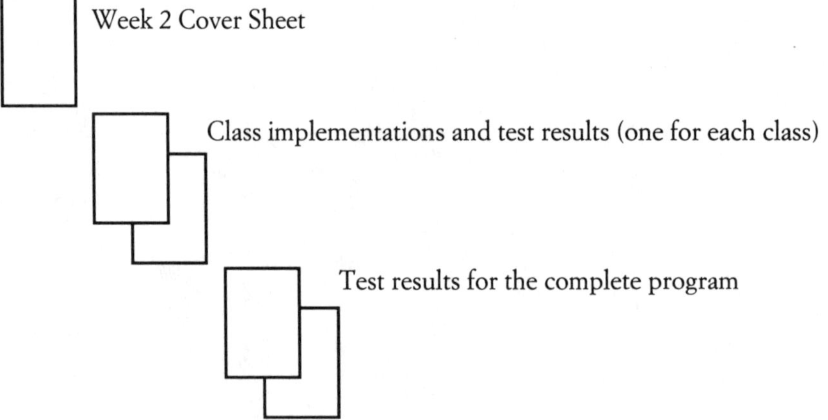

Test Plan for the Programming Project			
Test case	*Sample data*	*Expected result*	*Checked*

Laboratory 14: Postlab Exercise

PROJECT ANALYSIS

Date .... Section ....

Name ....

What problems did you face in implementing your class designs? What caused these problems? How would you avoid these kinds of problems in future programming efforts?